Watch Your Words

How we should use our words to speak faith, victory and prosperity instead of evil, lack and discouragement

by Montezz Allen

Watch Your Words

ISBN: 9781521388969

THANKS A LOT!

This is the first book I've ever written; to that, I'm thankful.

First and foremost, I'd like to dedicate this book to God. Without Him none of this is possible. I thank You for allowing creative ideas to invade my mind, for giving me the ability to write, and finally, for giving me the grace and patience to complete this book. Your grace is sufficient. You work in mysterious ways, but I understand all things will always work together for good for those who love and seek after You.

Also, I dedicate this book to my family. I don't know where I'd be if it wasn't for your support. You've stood by me through thick and thin. Words can't explain how much I love and care for you. My mother, step-father, sister, brother—everyone! Thank you so much for your support and unconditional love. It means a lot to me! You all give me the motivation to succeed every day. I will not stop. I promise to continue working toward being the best Montezz that I can possibly be. You've raised a man who's determined to make a positive impact on this world. My mission won't stop until I've done so. Thank you so much for your tough love, life-lessons and wisdom. I don't take it for granted.

Auntie Carnetta Witt, this book is dedicated to you as well. In 2012, right after I was accepted into DePaul University's graduate program, you took me in when I needed to move to Chicago. You didn't even think twice about it. I lived with you for four great years. You taught me so many life lessons — things that I'll keep with me for the rest of my life. Before you went to be with the Lord, I told you that I was going to be successful. I'm keeping that promise. Although you're not here with me physically, I'll always keep you close to my heart. You were the strongest woman I knew. Rest in paradise!

Last but not least, I dedicate this book to you — the reader. I want to encourage you all to watch your words. Watch what you speak into existence. Spread love, not hate. Encourage, don't discourage. Kill with kindness. Thank you all for your love and support.

SPREAD LOVE, NOT HATE

THE PREFACE

Do you know your words have creative power? I'm talking about power beyond your wildest dreams. The words you speak can determine the type of life you live. They can heal, uplift, or conversely, destroy, discourage and more.

I have a story to tell. It's ultimately what inspired me to write this book. You'll see why by the end of it.

Here it is.

One Friday I decided to have a few drinks at a bar in downtown Chicago. While there, I struck up a random conversation with this older guy. He was 53. Keep in mind I was only 28 at the time. Yeah, he was old enough to be my daddy.

After a few minutes of small talk, we got on the topic of family members passing away and going to be with the Lord. This guy had recently lost his mother. Once he was finished telling me his story something extraordinary happened. I believe it was divinely orchestrated.

Something began to rise up inside of me. I began to speak favor and prosperity into his life, slowly lifting his spirits.

Here's what I said:

"I know what you're going through is hard. You only get one mother and you were blessed to have one. I know it sounds cliché, but everything really does happen for a reason. God is in control of your life and all of our lives for that matter. We may not ever know why things happen. Only God knows. Many times He'll never reveal it to us.

"But just know that this is not the end of your story. God still has a great plan for your life. All things will work together for good for those who love Him. This is just one piece of the puzzle. One ingredient. Your mother loved you. She finished her course and God called her home. To be absent from the body is to be present with the Lord. She's home! You're blessed and make sure you continue to be a blessing to others."

Friends, when I say this man started weeping, I mean tears were flowing like the water at Niagara Falls. Mind you, we were in the middle of a crowded bar. There were people everywhere and he was crying like a baby. But he didn't care. The words I spoke over him had such an impact that he couldn't help himself.

Afterward, I said — not out loud, but to myself — "Wow! Here's this grown, 53-year-old man weeping because of me — a 28-year-old guy — prophesying and speaking life into his spirit." I didn't know him from a can of paint. I knew how words could have such a huge impact, but this reassured me of how powerful words can truly be when used properly. I knew right then that I had to tell the world how important words were. That's why I'm writing this book.

Enjoy!

CONTENTS

UPLIFT

ENCOURAGE

CHAPTER 1: LIFE AND DEATH IS IN THE POWER OF THE TONGUE

21 *"The tongue has the power of life and death, and those who love it will eat its fruit." Proverbs 18:21*

Think about that for a second. The words you speak can produce life or death. How powerful is that?

Let's check out how this can come true in a positive light.

I'm reminded of a man whose dream was to become an actor. On March 27, 1975, when he was 20-years-old, he was chilling in a beauty shop with his mother. While there, he caught an elderly lady staring at him. It was a strong gaze too — almost creepy-like. Can you imagine seeing a person staring at you like you've slapped their momma? Weird right?

Anyway, after staring for a while, she asked if someone could give her a piece of paper. They handed her the paper and she began writing on it. When she finished, she handed the young man the sheet of paper and it said this: "You will speak to millions of people and travel the world and preach to millions of people."

The young man had no idea what the lady was talking about. He probably thought she was insane, off her rocker and anything else you want to add.

Well…sane or insane, Denzel Washington is now one of the greatest, most accomplished actors of all time. He travels the world and touches millions of people through his acting and philanthropy.

Years after his run-in with the lady, Washington asked his pastor, "Do you think I should become a preacher?" His pastor responded: "That's what you're doing already."

See, his pastor believed his success as an actor was directly linked to what the lady prophesied back when she wrote those powerful words on that sheet of paper.

That elderly lady used her words — not verbally — but on paper, to prophesy Washington's future. Those words. Words of faith. Words of prosperity. Those strong words written on that sheet of paper touched Washington's spirit. It lit a fire under him. And now, he's living out that prophecy. Who would've thought a few simple sentences written down on a sheet of paper could have such a major impact.

The words we speak have creative power ladies and gentleman. The universe hears them. Your subconscious mind absorbs them and will manifest the words into reality, so be careful!

Watch your words!

Be conscience of what you speak into the atmosphere. It's extremely possible it may come to fruition. There's incredible power in what you cast out of your tongue.

Unfortunately, the world is full of negativity and hatred. People are so ugly toward one another. We tend not to take into account how the words we speak over people can either affect their lives for better or worse.

My question to you is why not? Why not spread love instead of hate? Why not cast out darkness with light? Why not uplift one another as much as possible?

You never know what a person is going through. Life is hard, unpredictable and it can beat you down to your knees if you let it. People don't want to hear negativity. It hurts the soul and dries the bones.

Negative words are like sharp knives. They penetrate and cut deep. They slowly kill the spirit.

On the contrary though, kind words are sweet to the soul. Metaphorically speaking, they make love to the soul. After all, who doesn't like being encouraged or spoken highly of? No one I've ever met! People like to be encouraged and complimented. It gives them confidence, motivation and tenacity.

So, without further ado, let me take a moment to encourage you!

CHAPTER 2: YOUR ENCOURAGEMENT

24 *"Gracious words are a honeycomb, sweet to the soul and healing to the bones." Proverbs 16:24*

Pleasant words do the body good like fruits and vegetables. That's why I want to take a moment to give you some encouragement if no one has done so already.

Why? I'm glad you asked. It's because you absolutely deserve it.

Are you ready? OK.

Three…two…one…let's go!

If nobody has told you, let me tell you. You're smart, talented, handsome, pretty, cute, intelligent and fearfully and wonderfully made. You have everything it takes to reach your dreams and live an Ephesians 3:20 life!

If you're not familiar with that verse, here you go…

20 **"Now to him who is able to do immeasurably more than all we ask or imagine, according to his power that is at work within us…"**

That's right. You have everything it takes to live an abundant life. More than enough. To lend and not borrow. To be the head and NOT the tail. You have the right personality, the perfect height and shape, the right looks — everything! Do NOT let anyone tell you otherwise. God made you how you are on purpose. He didn't create you and then scratch his head and say, "Oops, I made a mistake."

No!

He threw away the mold when He created you. You are His only copy. You're an original.

No clones!

When He finished creating you He took a step-back and said, "BAM! You're off the chain!" OK, probably not "off the chain," but you get my drift, ha-ha.

The world wants to put you into a box. It says you should look like this, act like that, be this size, have this type of hairstyle, do this job, etc.

Don't listen to those lies.

Yes, we live on this place called earth, but we're not from here. That's why Romans 12:2 says, 2 *"Do not conform to the pattern of this world, but be transformed by the renewing of your mind. Then you will be able to test and approve what God's will is— his good, pleasing and perfect will."*

You have talents and abilities you haven't even discovered yet. Things that you don't even know you can do. However, the seeds of greatness within you will not come out on their own. You have to develop them first. Trust me, I didn't know I could write a book until I just sat down, planned it and started writing!

You may be sitting back and saying to yourself, "Montezz, I don't have any great talents. I'm just a regular person."

Don't believe those lies!

Your greatness is hidden inside of you like treasure.

7 *"But we have this treasure in jars of clay to show that this all-surpassing power is from God and not from us."*
2 Corinthians 4:7

Nothing about you is regular. The enemy wants to deceive you, but don't deposit that junk into your spirit account. All of us have a divine destiny. God gave all of us a specific gift and assignment to complete. We have a purpose for being here. We shouldn't be going through life like zombies with no real goals, dreams or aspirations. Just going through life on auto-pilot, not trying to shake things up.

No! God has a plan.

Here's proof.

11 *"For I know the plans I have for you," declares the LORD, "plans to prosper you and not to harm you, plans to give you hope and a future." Jeremiah 29:11*

What God has in store for your life is amazing, but you have to receive it. Trust Him. Meet Him halfway. Do your part to reach this abundant life. Develop your greatness!

The people you see on TV who've reached greatness are NO different from you and I. They don't have some type of special power or magic within their bodies. They're human just like you! The only difference is that they took the time to be still and think. They highlighted their strengths. And then, they took time to discover their purpose, develop their talents and then tapped into it.

If they can achieve greatness then so can you! You may think what you have is insignificant. You might say, "Montezz, I don't have the best personality, I'm not as smart as my coworker, attractive like my best friend or talented like my sister or brother."

No, take that barrier off of your mind right now. You have everything you need to be successful. Again, God made you how you are on purpose. Nobody can be you better than you! You're already unique in that aspect. Think about it — there's only one you. No other person has your same look, fingerprint or personality. You're extremely special. I thank God for your existence. The world will never be the same after you're called home to your creator.

Know that you're great even before you reach greatness. Believe in yourself. Remember, your thoughts and words will manifest into reality if you continue to speak them into the universe. You're a winner. You're blessed and highly favored. You have what it takes. Shake off the intimidation, shake off the negative mindset, shake off the insecurities.

The enemy's goal is to steal, kill and destroy. But his primary objective is to control your mind. He understands how powerful the mind is and once he gets to it he'll be able to control your entire life!

The enemy will bombard your thoughts with nothing but negativity, lack and defeat. You know, thoughts like: *you've made too many mistakes. You're not smart enough to start your own business. You're too old. You don't have the money. How do you expect to get that management position when you're not qualified? You're washed up.* So on and so forth.

Am I right?

Take the lid off of what you think you can't achieve. Don't entertain those lies. Whenever thoughts of lack, negativity and defeat cross your mind, I want you to delete them quick, fast and in a hurry.

After you clean out those toxic thoughts, I want you to focus on what God says you should meditate on. And if you don't know, I'll be more than happy to share it with you.

8 *"Finally, brothers and sisters, whatever is true, whatever is noble, whatever is right, whatever is pure, whatever is lovely, whatever is admirable — if anything is excellent or praiseworthy — think about such things." Philippians 4:8*

Notice the difference between what God says you should meditate on versus the lies the enemy wants you to focus on.

It's like night and day, right? Of course it is.

Protect your thoughts my friends. Don't be deceived by the enemy. He wants you to live in mediocrity. He wants you to go through life depressed. Most of all, he wants to steal your joy! Life is too short for you to drag through the day sad, defeated; worried about your future, worried if you'll be able to pay your bills, worried if you will do anything great. God has already promised that you will. You have to believe and receive it!

The way you come out victorious is to simply dump out the negativity and move forward. Just delete it like a misspelled word. You have everything you need to triumph, so go out and do your thang!

Tackle the world head on. If it's hard then do it hard. Nothing comes easy. As the saying goes, easy come, easy go. If it were easy, everyone would do it. If you do what's easy then life will become hard, but if you do what's hard, life will become easy.

You are blessed and highly favored. Never forget that. Nothing can stop you. You've been crowned with favor from almighty God — the same God that flung stars into space, feeds the birds of the air and calms the seas. Is there anything too hard for Him?

Better yet, how about we quote scripture on this one: 26 **"Then the word of the LORD came to Jeremiah:** 27 **'I am the LORD, the God of all mankind. Is anything too hard for me?'" Jeremiah 32:26-27**

If you're reading this book, I want you to remember His favor lasts for a lifetime. Keep that in mind in your everyday walk with Him. Never forget. Never lose sight.

CHAPTER 3: SPEAK IT INTO EXISTENCE

17 "As it is written: 'I have made you a father of many nations.' "He is our father in the sight of God, in whom he believed — the God who gives life to the dead and calls into being things that were not.'" Romans 4:17

My brothers and sisters, our words are filled with so much power and conviction that we can literally call things into reality without seeing an inkling of a sign that it's going to come true. Pay attention to the last eight words of this verse - ***"and calls into being things that were not."***

You have to call things into existence that don't even exist yet. But here's the key: you must have FAITH that it'll come to pass. It's not going to happen overnight, but it will become a reality sooner or later if you have faith and patience.

I can hear you now. "Come on now, Montezz. That's God. He can do those things."

Very true. I'm not disputing that. I'm not saying you can go to a gravesite of one of your loved ones and say, "Rise up!" and they'll rise. That'll be pretty creepy. Plus, I wouldn't want the earth to turn into a land of zombies like an episode of the *Walking Dead.*

Let's be realistic. I'm talking about your goals and dreams. Something you're really aiming to accomplish with all of your heart.

Here's an example.

Growing up, ever since I can remember, I've always wanted to get a master's degree. I didn't know why, but I just knew I wanted one.

I was speaking it into existence since elementary school and I didn't even realize it. I'd say, "I'm going to get a master's degree someday. I know I am. Watch what I tell you." I didn't even know why I wanted a master's degree, but I just knew deep down inside that I wanted to earn one.

Well, in 2014, I was blessed enough to earn a Master of Arts in Journalism from DePaul University's College of Communication program. I was the first person in my immediate family to earn not only a bachelor's degree, but also a master's degree. The dream I had in me since I was a child finally came true.

Honestly, I truly believe it was because I called something that didn't yet exist, into existence, as though it already did exist. All it took was faith, patience, hard work, confidence and persistence.

That's it!

Was it difficult? Yes! Did I ever think about giving up? Yes! But it ended up being well worth it. It was worth the frustration, late-night cram sessions, pulling all-nighters — everything.

What am I trying to say?

It all started with my words — with something I spoke over my life in elementary school. If it can happen for me, it can happen for you too!

Believe deep down inside what you're confessing will come to pass. Envision it. Meditate on it day and night. Visualize it. Your subconscious mind translates things into pictures or visuals. See yourself doing whatever you want to do. Once you see yourself doing it, speak it. And then speak it some more! The universe will begin to send opportunities your way that will get you closer to your goal.

I want you to read what Jesus taught his disciples in Mark Chapter 11:23-24.

23 "Truly I tell you, if anyone says to this mountain, 'Go, throw yourself into the sea,' and does not doubt in their heart but believes that what they say will happen, it will be done for them. 24 Therefore I tell you, whatever you ask for in prayer, believe that you have received it, and it will be yours.'"

That's amazing. It's also a promise. And God always keeps His promises.

Jesus proclaims whatever you ask for in prayer you shall receive if you don't doubt. Just have faith. Mountain moving faith. Faith that no matter how long it takes, no matter how impossible the situation looks, no matter the opposition, it will come to reality if you do NOT doubt. Even when you don't see a way, have faith. God will make a way.

"Montezz, do you really think I can move mountains with my words? Like I said before, that's God. He can do those things."

Again, I'm not saying you can speak to the Appalachian Mountain, tell it to move and it will jump higher than Michael Jordan in a dunk contest.

No!

However, I look at the mountain as a metaphor. The mountain can be your finances, your health, a job you're believing for, a relationship — things of that nature. Instead of speaking about your situation, Jesus is saying speak to your situation, and then back it up with unwavering faith. You'll see a shift.

The key is to NOT doubt what you're praying for. After all, what's the point of praying for something if you're going to doubt and/or worry about what you're praying for? That makes no sense. Have unwavering faith. The type of faith that somehow, someway, what you're believing for will come true without a doubt.

Have this resolve about yourself. If not, it could possibly limit what God wants to do. You simply have to know, that you know, that you know!

In James 1:6-8, it actually warned us of how our doubts can limit what God can do.

6 "But when you ask, you must believe and not doubt, because the one who doubts is like a wave of the sea, blown and tossed by the wind. 7 That person should not expect to receive anything from the Lord. 8 Such a person is double-minded and unstable in all they do."

That's some powerful stuff right there. I don't know about you, but I don't want to block anything that's good and wholesome because of something as simple as having doubt. And yes, I understand we're all human. Doubt comes to our minds all the time, especially when you don't see a way out of the situation you're currently in. It can be tough and I get that. Shoot, doubt creeps into my mind all the time too. Many times you just can't help it.

On the other hand, when it does slither into your mind like a rattlesnake, you have to cast it out immediately. Don't let it take root. The more you let it settle there, the more you'll start believing it and then you'll talk yourself out of whatever you're believing for. View doubt as a common cold.

When you start to become ill, you feel the symptoms before they get worse, whether it may be a sore throat, a slight headache or cough.

What do you do next?

Most people try to nip it in the bud. You take medicine, drink lots of tea, orange juice, water, get plenty of rest, etc.

Well, treat doubt the same way. As soon as it starts to creep in, nip it in the bud right away before it gets out of hand. Instead of meditating on what the enemy is trying to place into your mind, take your medicine (God's promises) and fight it! When your thoughts start to tell you you're not good enough to get that new position. Respond with, "No! I'm blessed and highly favored. I can do all things through Christ who strengthens me."

Or, when they say nothing good will ever happen to you, turn it around and say, "God's favor surrounds me like a shield, His blessings are chasing me down and I deserve to have good things happen to me."

Always try to choose the right words. Watch your tongue. The universe is listening to everything you say. I know it sounds weird, but it's a fact. Prophesy positivity, life, abundance and prosperity.

If you begin to do this, you'll start to see your life flow in a different direction. Things will begin to shift.

Practice it. What do you have to lose?

Just do it!

CHAPTER 4: WATCH WHAT YOU SAY ABOUT YOURSELF

4 "The soothing tongue is a tree of life, but a perverse tongue crushes the spirit." Proverbs 15:4

My brothers and sisters, learn to tame your tongue. Think before you speak. Like it says in the verse above, a perverse tongue can CRUSH the spirit. The word "crush" stands out like a sore thumb to me. It means to destroy, flatten or subdue. Each one of those words has a negative connotation attached to it. That's how powerful your words can be. They have the ability to CRUSH someone's spirit.

That reminds me of a sermon the great pastor, author and motivational speaker, Joel Osteen wrote some years ago. As some of you may know, Joel Osteen pastors Lakewood Church in Houston, Texas.

Mr. Osteen wrote a sermon entitled, "The Power of I AM." That particular sermon truly resonated with me. In it, he claimed whatever follows your I AM will ultimately determine the outcome of your life. For example, if you go around saying, "I am dumb, I am unattractive, I am broke, I am never going to make it out of the hood…" — all of those things will come looking for you! You're inviting them into your spirit whether you realize it or not.

I agree with his claim 1,000 percent. The things you consistently say about yourself will eventually hunt you down like the way bloodhounds hunt down escaped convicts.

It's absolutely imperative that you constantly be mindful of what you say and think about yourself. After all, how can you expect to live a life full of victory if you're always speaking defeat, lack and insecurity into the atmosphere? You won't!

Instead, you'll keep taking L's.

Never be afraid to encourage yourself. Do it daily. When you wake up in the morning, take a good look in the mirror, and begin to speak great things about yourself. Speak favor and prosperity into your future. Many times we don't even realize what we're saying about ourselves. It's almost like we're immune to it.

Quit being so negative. Quit beating yourself up. Use your words wisely. It takes the same amount of energy to focus your energy on the positive as it does for the negative.

Instead of saying, "I'm not talented, I'm so old, I can't do anything great." Or, "I'm fat, I'm out of shape, I'm terrible at my job," turn it around. Speak the things that God says about you.

"I'm fearfully and wonderfully made. I am a masterpiece. Everything I touch will prosper and succeed. Blessings are chasing me down. I'm equipped to handle any and everything. If God be for me, then who dare be against me?"

Let's take it even further.

"I'm handsome, I'm fine, intelligent and equipped to succeed in life. I have the favor of the Lord on my life. I'm healthy. I'm living in abundance. I can do all things through Christ who strengthens me."

Those words are sweet to your soul. They'll uplift your spirit. Your life will follow your thoughts along with what comes out of your mouth.

That reminds me of a story comedian and actor Jim Carrey told Oprah Winfrey during an interview on her show back on February 17,1997. His dream was to become a famous actor. At the time, he didn't have two pennies to rub together. He was broke. But he still had a dream. He knew deep down inside he was going to accomplish his God-given dream of becoming a famous actor.

Carrey told how every night he would go out on Mulholland Drive in Southern California to fantasize and visualize the things he wanted — fame, fortune and starring in hit movies.

"I had nothing at that time," Carrey said, "but, it just made me feel better. At that time, all it really was for me was kind of making me feel better. I would drive home and say, 'I do have these things. I don't have ahold of them yet, but they're out there.'"

Carrey did something else that I found to be extremely valuable. He wrote himself a check for $10 million dollars for "Acting Service Rendered" and then prophesied the amount of time it would take him to make that amount of cash. He then dated it for Thanksgiving of 1995.

Sure enough, just before Thanksgiving of 1995, Carrey found out he was going to make $10 million dollars off the movie *Dumb and Dumber.*

What was Carrey doing?

He was prophesying his own future via his thoughts and words.

Although he didn't physically have what he was believing for in his personal possession, he knew 100 percent he'd eventually get those things in due time. Carrey called things that were not as though they already existed.

People, if you see it in your mind, you can touch it with your hand. You have the ability to turn the vision you see in your head into a monetary equivalent. You have the power within you to make it a reality.

Steve Harvey, a very successful actor, comedian, radio and TV host, once said in one of his shows, "Science says show me and then I'll believe, but faith says believe and then I'll show you."

You attract what you fear. You attract what you speak. Most importantly, if you believe and have faith, you can attract the desires of your heart if you're willing to put in the work. All of us have the ability to speak and think things into existence. That's why it's extremely important to encourage yourself. Speak great things about yourself. If you won't, no one else will!

UFC mixed martial artist Jon "Bones" Jones also understood this principle. His dream was to become the youngest UFC champion in the sport's history. Before his light heavyweight bout with Mauricio "Shogun" Rua in 2011, Jones had been signing "champ 2011" on almost every autograph people had asked him for.

But that's not all.

Jones revealed something in an interview before his fight. The reporter asked, "A lot of people were surprised when they found out that you've been signing your name as champ 2011. How did that come about?"

Jones' answer was interesting.

His response: "I believe in the law of attraction. I believe that you can speak things into existence. And I believe that when you know where you're going and you know what you want, the universe has a way of stepping aside for you. Me signing my signature as champ 2011 on it can't hurt me."

Sure enough, Jones ended up winning the light heavyweight championship in March 2011 over Rua and accomplished his goal of becoming the youngest champion in UFC history. He saw his dream come true.

How did he do it?

Obviously, his talent was a big part of it. I won't discredit the amount of time, effort and discipline he put into his craft. Fighting in the UFC is no joke. The toll it takes on the human body can be ridiculous — the training regime, diet, sacrifice. It's all extremely difficult to endure, but he kept at it. More importantly, he believed in himself and called the things that were not as though they already were.

Conversely, if Jones had became a slave to the negative thoughts bombarding his mind (and yes, he did have them because he's human), meditating on the bad instead of the positive, the outcome would've been much different. He would've lost the battle before it even began.

I understand nothing is guaranteed. That's a given. But I will say his chances of winning the match increased considerably because of his mindset. That was a major key and it played an important factor in his success.

Think about it: prior to his fight with Rua, if he had been going around thinking and spewing thoughts of defeat, thoughts of uncertainty and inferiority — those thoughts would've more than likely became his reality. Jones was wise enough to accept this principle. He understood how his words could determine the outcome of certain situations.

Since his dream was to become the youngest UFC lightweight champ in the history of the sport, he didn't want to do anything to jeopardize his chances of winning.

My friends, a lot of things in your life are a consequence of how you think, paired with what you speak.

Remember that!

CHAPTER 5: SPEAK LIFE INTO ONE ANOTHER

*17 "As iron sharpens iron, so one person sharpens another."
Proverbs 27:17*

The book of Proverbs is a book of knowledge and wisdom.

Brothers and sisters, if you never read a single book in the Bible, at the very least, please read the book of Proverbs. It's short and the lessons you'll learn are invaluable. It's the type of wisdom that guides you through this thing called life.

"As iron sharpens iron, so one person sharpens another."

Just let that sink into your spirit for a minute. Think to yourself what this verse really means.

In the meantime, I'm going to reveal another story to you.

At one point in my life, I had to drive Uber to make some extra cash on the side. Times were a little hard, so I had to do what I had to do.

Believe it or not, I met some pretty interesting people while driving Uber — people who had traveled the world, won gold medals in the Olympics, all sorts of amazing things.

I remember one afternoon, I picked up a young lady at a bus stop near the West Side of Chicago.

She attended college in that part of the city. It wasn't too far from the bus stop. Not too long after she got in the car, she and I struck up a conversation. A good one too. I hated driving and not conversing with the passengers. It was too awkward. My thought process was you never know who you're speaking with.

This girl was on her way to class. We talked about everything from what she was studying in school, to how she planned on accomplishing her goals.

About 10 minutes into the ride, I told her I was in the process of writing a book and how it was my first attempt at trying to write one.

She asked what the book was about. I went on to explain the premise. By looking at her facial expressions, I could tell that my ideas really touched her. It was like a lightbulb had come on.

What she said to me afterward was fascinating. She said, "I know what you mean. When I was a child, I had some negative things spoken over my life that I still battle with to this day. You're right! Your words do have power."

I couldn't believe it. Talk about perfect timing. The quote the young woman gave me in the back of my car was the epitome of why we should sharpen each other with our words.

This young woman was still battling some of the titles people slapped on her as a child. It's almost as if those words had a stronghold on her. They literally pierced her mind and soul.

Speaking of piercing. Here's a proverb that warns us of how words can pierce our spirit.

18 *"The words of the reckless pierce like swords, but the tongue of the wise brings healing." Proverbs 12:18*

Wow!

Let's break down the first part: *"The words of the reckless pierce like swords..."*

Words can be so devastating, so discouraging and so harmful that they can impale your mind, body and spirit like a sword. That means the words people let flow out their mouths can cut very deep.

Things like: you'll never do anything in life. Your personality is whack. You don't have enough talent.

Saying such things can scar a person, badly. Sometimes it can have a dramatic effect on how that particular person lives out the rest of their life.

The good news is that the verse doesn't cut off at *"pierce like swords."* It gets better. The verse then goes on to say *"but the tongue of the wise brings healing."*

Healing is the word that stands out.

If we start to use our words to encourage and uplift like we're supposed to, then they can bring healing. Soothe pain. Lift up. Sharpen.

When you're at work and you see a coworker doing a great job, give that person a compliment. Tell them how good of a job they're doing. Let them know how talented they are.

Life happens to all of us. You never know what someone is going through. Those small words of encouragement and positivity can bring joy and healing. You can easily make someone's day by speaking words that bring healing and comfort.

I look at my own life as an example. I work in the TV and radio business. A very competitive business. There are so many talented people. The array of anchors and reporters I come across are simply amazing. Much more talented than me.

Do I get jealous or intimidated? No. Threatened because of their skill-level or success?

No way!

Other people's success shouldn't threaten you. It should motivate you.

I've been blessed to attend what's called NABJ conventions. NABJ stands for the National Association of Black Journalists.

It's an all-black organization filled with thousands of talented media professionals. NABJ hosts an annual convention in different cities.

Media professionals from all over the country come to fellowship, network, job hunt, party, and gain additional knowledge through various workshops and panels.

If I had to take a guess, I'd say I don't know more than 80 percent of the people that I come across during the conventions. But that doesn't matter to me.

Regardless if we've never met, I always make an effort to sharpen each and every person I come across.

Why?

Well for starters, you never know who you're talking to. You could possibly be entertaining someone who could open a door that will help you get closer to your destiny. Or, you could hit it off, develop a strong relationship and before you know it, you have a life-long friend. You just never know.

That's why it's extremely important to make a deposit. Sharpen people with your words.

I'll give you an example.

The 2016 NABJ convention was held in Washington, D.C., a place I had never been. D.C. is a beautiful city. The people are welcoming, the food is pretty good and the weather is legit. Plus, it's a tourist attraction. There are so many monuments and museums to check out. I'd definitely recommend going if you've never been.

As far as the convention goes, I constantly ran into people I've never seen before. There are so many journalists that it's impossible to meet everyone. You'd have to be a networking fool.

Here's the point: I made a conscience effort to speak prosperity into every single person I came in contact with. I didn't care if you were already established in your career or just starting out. Everyone got it.

With every person I met, I made sure to tell them how good of a job they were doing and how they have what it takes. And no matter what happens, keep their eye on the prize. Nothing special, just a few words of encouragement.

Again, you never know who you're speaking to at these type of conventions. It's important to touch any and every person's life you come across. It doesn't necessarily have to be a physical gift. Some simple words of encouragement can go a long way.

Here's how to do the exact opposite of what Proverbs 27:17 says.

This one comes from a personal experience of mine.

Graduating from DePaul University's College of Communication program in 2014 was probably the biggest accomplishment of my life at the time. I completed the criteria to earn a master's degree. Not only that, I was the first person out of my immediate family to have a degree, period — let alone two of them.

The next thing on my list was to land a job. Little did I know, that was coming too. I kid you not. I was at graduation, walking down the ramp and headed toward the stage when one of my former classmates and I linked up. He told how he had got hired as a production assistant at a startup digital sports network in Chicago.

He was hired in about a week or so before the graduation.

Of course I told him congratulations and what a blessing it was to land a job before we graduated. We continued talking about the position for a while, the details of what it demanded, its location, etc.

He then said he'll give me the contact information to one of the hiring managers.

About a week after the ceremony, I reached out to that manager. To my surprise, it didn't take long for me to get a reply back. I'd say about a week to be exact. In his email, he asked if I wanted to take a tour of the building.

I definitely couldn't turn that down, so I agreed.

In my mind, it was on. Game time. Game 7 to be exact. This was my opportunity to land a job right out of graduate school. That's rare. Sometimes it takes college grads years to land a job in their respective field.

I knew that, so I had to go into Black Mamba mode.

What's that you ask? Let me educate you real quick.

For those who don't know me personally, I'm a huge Kobe Bryant fan. He's my Michael Jordan. I was born in 1988 so I caught the tail end of MJ.

Kobe Bryant always brought his A-game no matter what. He had this mentality where he was going to destroy any opponent on the basketball court. It didn't matter if it was in practice or the All-Star game. He was going to kill you like the venomous snake "Black Mamba."

I couldn't blow it. I had to put on the MAMBA MENTALITY and kill the interview.

Fast forward to the tour. I can't remember exactly what day it was on, but I do remember I could barely sleep the night before. I was excited and nervous at the same time.

I woke up early too. The interview wasn't until the afternoon, but I woke up super early anyway.

How can you blame me? It was a chance to land my first real, full-time job out of graduate school.

I finally arrived at the building. The nerves weren't that bad, but they still were there.

The receptionist was expecting me. I told her my name and who I was. She seemed more excited than I did.

After waiting for about 15 minutes, I was approached by the hiring manager. He took me on a tour of the building, including the studio. I was amazed. Ecstatic. In awe. Whatever positive word you want to put to it, I was that.

When the tour was over, we ended up in his office where the interview was set to take place. "Mamba mentality" I thought to myself. I was prepared. Focused. Locked in!

The interview was over before I knew it. I was confident I had made a great impression.

Everything about it just felt right.

I was right!

Two weeks later, while I was in the computer lab at DePaul, I got a call. It was the hiring manager.

He offered me the job! I wanted to breakdance like it was the 80s or something. I had just landed a job straight out of graduate school. On top of that, it was in my field too! It was an exciting time. Little did I know, I was in for a rude awakening.

This, my friends, is where the story gets interesting.

It took about a month for me to start. Anxious wasn't the word. I couldn't wait. But if I knew what was coming, I would've rejected the job. But God allows you to go through things so you'll have a testimony once it's over.

Before I finish the story, let me say I'm going to reframe from using the name of the company as well as the manager I'll be referring to. It's out of respect. Plus, I don't want to get sued, ha-ha.

Let's proceed…

My first day was filled with training. Two highly skilled production assistants were chosen to show me the ropes. I caught on pretty fast. I just knew I was going to excel.

My second day on the job I was handed my work computer and then was thrown into the fire. I felt ready though. I wasn't a bit nervous.

Here's where it gets interesting.

Throughout the course of my life, I've had some pretty cool supervisors. Bad ones too, but the majority of them were fine.

The one at this particular job easily won the award for the worst manager of all time!

Now, to give him the benefit of the doubt, I'll be honest. One of my dreams was to cover sports as a sports anchor and reporter. However, my sports knowledge when it came to baseball and hockey wasn't the best at the time.

As a production assistant, the job description was to watch my assigned games in a system called interplay. Depending on the season, I'd be covering baseball, basketball, college football, boxing, UFC, NASCAR, hockey and golf.

I would mark the best plays and then develop certain storylines from the game. In a sport like hockey or baseball, if someone scored a goal, hit a home run, etc., I'd mark that play, write a description of it, sit with an editor and then the on-air talent would read what I wrote over the air as an update.

As you can imagine, there wasn't much room for error. Whenever I had a typo, spelled a name wrong or got a score wrong, the on-air talent could see it and possibly trip up over the air.

My first day working under this supervisor from hell gave me a look into how the next year-and-a-half was going to be.

I was assigned one game on my second day. It was baseball. I can't remember who was playing.

An outfielder was up to bat. He drilled a home run to left field. My first update was on the way.

When a team scored, the goal was to get the play on-air as soon as possible. Move at the speed of Twitter was the motto. It was a pretty impossible motto, but hey, it's what the company lived by.

As I was writing my update, the manager from hell out of nowhere started screaming at me, saying, "Montezz. Hurry the hell up! Let's go. Get that on-air as soon as possible."

I jumped up, went to an editor and got the update on as fast as I could. As time went on, there would be more where that came from. But on another level.

Over the course of my first year at this new company, I made countless mistakes in my scripts. It still upsets me to this day. I'm talking about typo's, screwing up plays — the whole nine.

I was trying my best. It wasn't like I was doing it on purpose. It was just my learning period.

Before that job, I had never watched an entire game of baseball or hockey. Growing up in my hood, there was just football and basketball. As a result, it had limited my knowledge of those sports.

My writing reflected it.

But in the words of the late basketball coach John Wooden, "If you're not making mistakes, then you're not doing anything. I'm positive that a doer makes mistakes."

Before I knew it, my first year at the company was coming to an end and the dreaded review was coming up. To be honest, I thought I was doing well. I felt like I was improving every day. Learning from my mistakes. I wasn't receiving any feedback from the managers, so I figured I was in good standing.

Not!

I was so used to being the guy excelling at almost everything I did. I was used to being one of the top workers, students, athletes, whatever it was, I was accustomed to being one of the best.

So during my review, when I was told I was doing a horrible job, my sports knowledge was below average and I was looked at as a lower production assistant, I was devastated. The words spoken over me really had a huge impact.

I felt like a failure.

Afterward, I felt the need to prove them wrong. I had a major chip on my shoulder. But it got worse. No matter what I did, my work was never acknowledged.

On top of that, the manager I was working under started to verbally abuse me on almost a daily basis.

One day, I was assigned a Baltimore Orioles game. The game was pretty dry. There wasn't too much going on. I'm talking about groundouts, RBI singles — just a horrible game.

Once the game had came to an end, I reached out to the highlight supervisor so he could help me form a storyline. He told me what I should write my recap on. I followed his instruction, finished my recap, sat down with an editor and then sent it down to the talent.

About 15 minutes later, my supervisor came out of his office and asked, "Who had the Orioles highlight?"

I thought to myself, "Awww shoot, here we go." I then raised my hand and told him the highlight was mine.

Mind you, before he went off on a tangent, the office was filled with other production assistants. There were probably about 10 of us that day. Let's just say they witnessed everything.

Let's continue…

After I let him know I cut the Orioles highlight, he went off! The verbal abuse got absolutely real!

It went a little something like this: "Who told you to cut this highlight? You think people want to see three RBI singles. Know your weaknesses. You just don't know the game, period. You just don't have what it takes to cover baseball. This is absolutely horrible."

That was just the tip of the iceberg. Most people would've lost it and retaliated. Me, I just sat there and took it on the chin. I tried my hardest to ignore him. I definitely wanted to get up out of my chair and slap him though. But that's not the point.

That wasn't the end of it.

More of the same went on. There were plenty of times where he told me I didn't have what it took to be on-air as a Sports Anchor/Reporter. That I was getting worse and not better. For whatever reason this man was just against me.

Yes, I made mistakes. Yes, I felt dumb because of it. But did that give him the right to verbally abuse me over and over and over again?

Hell no!

I eventually got a part-time job as a Sports Anchor/Reporter just outside of Chicago. I was on-air ladies and gentleman. God is good. Here's what he said when he found out: "I've seen what you've done on-air, but that's nothing. Just wait until you get to a real station."

This went on for almost two years. I had never met a person so against me in my life. It got to a point where it rubbed off on a few other supervisors.

Here's the key: if I had been mentally weak, I would've let the words he spoke over me become my reality. Now I use them as motivation.

I realized he couldn't determine my destiny, only God can. He wasn't the author of my life, God is.

It was extremely tough. To hear someone belittle you almost every time you work is very stressful. I wouldn't wish that on my worst enemy. Work got tough and after a while I dreaded going in.
To my surprise, I was laid-off not too long after. The funny thing was that I wasn't mad at all. The working environment was horrible and I truly believe God knew I needed a change.

I appreciate that manager to this day. He did nothing but motivate me to achieve success. He was placed in my life to rub the rough edges off of me. Help me to become stronger. Better. More motivated than ever.

Thank you manager from hell. I really appreciate you!

CHAPTER 6: OPINIONS DON'T HAVE TO BECOME YOUR REALITY

29 "Do not let any unwholesome talk come out of your mouths, but only what is helpful for building others up according to their needs, that it may benefit those who listen." Ephesians 4:29

We've all heard the saying, "If you don't have anything nice to say, don't say it at all." It has been around since forever. The fact of the matter is, that saying is quite true. Nothing, and I mean nothing, should spill out of your mouth unless it's for the purpose of edifying or improvement, period!

What other people think and say about you can become your reality if you let it. However, if you don't let the negative words sink into your spirit, what others think and say about you will NOT come to fruition.

It took Les Brown — one of the greatest motivational speakers of our day— a long time to understand this principle.

If you're not familiar with Les Brown, know that the man is absolutely amazing. He's so talented and smart. His speeches will have you thinking you can run through a brick wall.

He has spoken all over the world in front of crowds as large as 80,000. He has spoken to Fortune 500 companies, CEO's and prison inmates. By his success, you'd think he was ordained with the ability to speak and influence others at an early age.

That couldn't be further from the truth.

At a young age, one particular teacher he met changed his entire outlook on life and helped unleash the Les Brown we see today.

Here's a story of how other people's opinions can shape your reality if you let what people say take root.

Les Brown along with his twin brother Wesley, were born on a floor in an abandoned building in Liberty City — a poverty-struck, low-income section of Miami, Florida.

Three weeks later, he and his brother were given up for adoption. They were eventually adopted by Ms. Mamie Brown at six weeks of age. She was an unmarried cafeteria cook.

Brown grew up poor. Mamie Brown didn't have much money, but she did the best she could. In fact, Brown will tell you, "Everything I am and everything I have I owe to my mother."

Brown struggled in school, especially when it came to reading. He was considered a poor student because of his lack of focus in the classroom. That, coupled with his teachers' inability to see his worth; he was slapped with the label, educable mentally retarded.

You may ask, "What does educable mentally retarded mean?" Well, an educable mentally handicapped student is one whose intellect and adaptive behavior is mildly impaired. Also, their development reflects a reduced rate of learning.

Brown was pushed back from the fifth grade to the fourth grade and then failed again in the eighth grade. He remained in the educable mentally retarded category until he graduated high school.

The opinions of others became his reality.

"They said I was slow, so I held to that pace," Brown said.

In short, he had a hard time removing the label, partly due to the fact that he didn't even try.

Brown attended Booker T. Washington High School in Miami, Florida. While there, something changed for him. And it was because of LeRoy Washington, a speech and drama instructor.

One day while in class waiting on another student, Washington came in and asked him to go to the board and work out a problem. "I can't do that, sir," Brown quickly responded. Washington then replied, "Why not?"

"Because I'm not one of your students," Brown said. Washington didn't care. He just wanted Brown to follow his instruction and go to the chalkboard. Brown wouldn't do it. Then he said something that pissed Washington completely off.

Brown said, "I can't do it because I'm educable mentally retarded."

Washington was shocked and appalled Brown would say something like that. He was so disturbed by his comment that he came from behind his desk and told him something that would eventually change his life forever.

Washington looked at Brown and said, "Don't ever say that again. Someone's opinion of you doesn't have to become your reality!"

That comment planted a seed in Brown's mind. It broke the spirit of discouragement, lack and low self-esteem.

You see, up until that point, Brown had been conditioned to think he was mentally handicapped because someone had put that label on him. It took a teacher to speak life and faith into his spirit to break that horrible label.

Imagine if Mr. Washington would've never gave Brown that advice. Imagine if he would've instead said, "Are you really? I would've never guessed. Now that I think of it, you do kind of look retarded. You're right. There's no need for you to write this down on the board. You're just not capable of doing it."

Instead, Mr. Washington understood how words can affect a person. He understood just because a person has a certain opinion of you doesn't mean their opinion is correct. Opinions are like buttholes, everybody has one.

The teachers that labeled young Les Brown educable mentally retarded obviously didn't consider Ephesians 4:29.

Nope.

Instead, that label crippled him for a long time until a teacher changed his way of thinking.

Now, I don't want you all to think I'm "holier than thou" because I'm not. Not even close. We're all human. We all fall short. We've all had things come out of our mouths that was in no way, shape or form beneficial to the person we were aiming the words toward. Whether it was out of anger, spite or jealousy – it doesn't matter.

I'm simply trying to raise awareness. I'm trying to make you more aware of what you're saying to yourself and others.

"Sticks and stones will break your bones, but words can never harm you." That's one of the most false sayings I've ever heard.

I've seen this in my life. Particularly when I was younger.

As a kid, basketball was my life. My goal, like many young, black kids growing up in the inner city, was to make it to the NBA.

I know what you're thinking. The chances of making it were slim, but I didn't care. I figured if other people could do it, why couldn't I?

All I did was play ball. From every recreation center, park playground, to elementary school, middle school and then high school. Believe it or not, I was really good. I mean really good. I'm still good to this day!

I had people telling me I was going to make it to the league and everything. Scouts were looking at me. I was ranked nationally. Not high, but at least I was ranked. The future was pretty bright.

I could shoot, dribble, pass and finish at the rim. I probably had the quickest first-step out of all the competition I faced in my time hooping. The only problem was this: my thinking sucked!

I was very small! Super small. Short and skinny with skill, that was me. But it didn't matter because I could ball.

Most of the time, I was the smallest player on the team. But the reason why I always made the team and eventually became the starting PG was because of my skill-set.

Here's the kicker though. And if I would've known this back then as a young, immature high school basketball player, I truly believe things would've turned out a bit differently.

I listened to the critics. Better yet, I believed the critics. I also didn't believe in myself.

I transitioned to high school in 10th grade. My middle school went from seventh to ninth grade. When I got there, I was a mere 5-foot-6 and about 115 pounds soak and wet, if that.

Again, I had all the skill in the world, but I listened to the whispers of the critics.

I was told I was too small and frail — and that I wouldn't make it to the next level because of my size.

I remember one player on varsity told me, "Tezz, you got the skill, man, but you're just too small. They're going to kill you when you start playing varsity." I tried my best to ignore it, but I made the mistake of letting those words sink into my spirit.

Mind you, while on JV (junior varsity), we used to scrimmage varsity all of the time. They were much bigger than us. More physical. Stronger. All of that. Funny thing was that it didn't faze me one bit.

I had the skill to compete with them. I may not have been the biggest or strongest at the time, but my skill-set made up for it.

Truth is, it took a long time for me to get over the words that varsity ball player spoke over me. It affected my confidence, self-esteem and focus. I knew I had the game, but I eventually began to believe that my lack of size would truncate my ability to make an impact on the hardwood.

Of course, that was a complete lie. Why? Because there were lots of other players my size who were successful in the high school ranks and eventually went on to play in college. Some even went on to play in the NBA.

Looking back, I know I had what it took. But like Les Brown, there was a stronghold in my mind that prevented me from accomplishing my goal of at least playing in college.

After high school, I went on to attend college at Oakland University. Home of the Grizzlies!

I was still very much in basketball playing shape, and of course, I was still really good!

My first day on campus I thought to myself, "I should try out for the basketball team."

One problem: my thoughts were telling me not to do it. I eventually talked myself out of it.

Perfect transition into the next chapter…

CHAPTER 7: THOUGHTS LEAD TO THINGS

7 "For as he thinketh in his heart, so is he: Eat and drink, saith he to thee; but his heart is not with thee." Proverbs 23:7

There's a battlefield going on in our minds. Your thoughts along with whatever you let flow out of your mouth go hand and hand. Your thoughts can either talk you out of things or convince you to take action.

Your thoughts can keep you happy or happily depressed. Your mind is the most powerful tool in your body. ***"For as he thinketh in his heart, so is he…"*** Your thoughts can shape your reality.

There's a great poem from the famous book entitled "Think & Grow Rich," written by Napoleon Hill. It really puts your thinking into perspective. Check it out…

"If you think you dare not, you don't
If you like to win, but you think you can't, It is almost certain
you won't.

"If you think you'll lose, you're lost

For out of the world we find, Success begins with a fellow's
will- It's all in the state of mind.

"If you think you are outclassed, you are, You've got to think
high to rise, You've got to be sure of yourself before You can
ever win a prize.

"Life's battles don't always go
To the stronger or faster man, But soon or late the man who
wins is the man WHO THINKS HE CAN!"

A famous quote by the great Henry Ford says, "Whether you think you can, or you think you can't, you're right."

Sit on that for a moment.

If you think you don't have what it takes to run that company, then you don't. You'll never run it. Simply because you don't think you can. If you think you don't have enough skill to make the basketball team, you don't.

On the contrary, deep down inside, if you truly believe you can, you will!

If you think success, you go success. If you think down, you go down. If you think up, you will go up. If you think you can, you will!

If you think you're not smart enough, you're not. If you think you can't ever reach your dreams, you won't.

Your thoughts pretty much determines the outcome of your entire life. I learned that the hard way during my days of playing basketball.

As I mentioned in the previous chapter, I honestly believe my basketball career ended because of my thoughts.

I had all the talent in the world, but I didn't believe in myself. It doesn't matter who believes in you. If you don't believe in you, it won't happen for you. You'll never achieve greatness.

My thoughts told me I wasn't good enough. My thoughts told me I didn't have the talent. My thoughts told me I was too small.

I didn't believe in myself so I gave up playing. Let me tell you. Before giving up basketball I didn't have a real regret in my life.

The feeling of regret is awful. In my short time on this earth, I can say I've tasted the likes of true regret. Giving up basketball, it's a terrible feeling.

I didn't go to any college basketball tryouts because I was too nervous. Afraid. Timid. I didn't believe in my mind that I was truly good enough.

Do you hear what I'm saying?

Negative thoughts can destroy your destiny.

Cover your mind. Cover your thoughts. Cover your destiny!

Some of you may say, "Now Montezz, even if you were good, you couldn't have made it to the NBA."

To that I say you just never know!

What about getting a full ride to a college to play ball? Eliminating school loans, which means a clean slate after graduation.

What about the doors that could've possibly opened after my college playing days were over?

Do you know how many basketball dreams I have to this day? Dreams I'm playing in the league, or at a college, in high school — everything!

Whether I would've made it to the NBA or not, the point is that negative thoughts can stop a plan God may have for your life. But that's why He's the God of more than enough. He puts other dreams into your heart, or, He can still bring your initial dream to pass.

Nothing's impossible with Him.

God never allows anything to happen to you unless there's a greater purpose for it. I think I learned that purpose. The lesson taught me to never let fear, lack of confidence or low self-esteem stop me from reaching my dreams ever again!

Friends, we're not always going to be here. The Bible says our lives are like a mist and then it vanishes.

James 4:14 puts it this way: 14 *"Why, you do not even know what will happen tomorrow. What is your life? You are a mist that appears for a little while and then vanishes."*

Life is too short to let your thoughts stop you from reaching an abundant life.

Don't let your mind talk you out of your destiny.

Les Brown said, "If you're nervous, do it nervous!"

Muhammad Ali — arguably the greatest boxer of all time — was notoriously known for his trash talk. Ali was so great at talking trash that even though it was trash talk, there still was a valuable message behind it all.

Ali once said: "I am the greatest, I said that even before I knew I was."

Ali didn't know from the jump, but he believed anyway. He convinced himself to believe he was the greatest boxer to ever grace the ring. Ali, a skinny, 6-foot-3 kid from Louisville, Kentucky, shocked the world when he — then known as Cassius Clay — beat Sonny Liston to win the world heavyweight championship at just 22-years-old in 1964.

Much of it was because of his thoughts. His thoughts allowed him to develop the work ethic to get up every morning to work on his stamina. His thoughts told him to hit the gym to work on his skills.

Most of all, his thoughts told him to pay the critics NO mind. If he believed in himself, he could shock the world.

I think Ali did a pretty good job of that. He died an icon.

It was all in his mind.

Speaking of the mind — again, in "Think & Grow Rich," Napoleon Hill talks about the power of the mind. He said if it's really made up, you can achieve anything and turn it into a monetary equivalent.

Yes, that means massive success in your finances.

Everybody wants more money.

Hill backed up his claim with plenty of examples. Off the top of my head, Thomas Edison was one.

Thomas Edison supposedly failed at creating the lightbulb 999 times. He dared to try one more time and created it on his 1,000th attempt. Boom! His life instantly changed.

Edison had his mind made up. There was no stopping him. He won because of his ability to persevere. Deep down inside he knew it was going to happen for him. You could NOT have convinced him otherwise.

"I have not failed. I've just found 10,000 ways that won't work." — Thomas A. Edison

Friends, thoughts are powerful.

How about that poem, huh?

"If you think you are beaten, you are, If you think you dare not, you don't
If you like to win, but you think you can't, It is almost certain you won't.

"If you think you'll lose, you're lost For out of the world we find, Success begins with a fellow's will- It's all in the state of mind.

"If you think you are outclassed, you are, You've got to think high to rise, You've got to be sure of yourself before You can ever win a prize.

"Life's battles don't always go

To the stronger or faster man, But soon or late the man who

wins Is the man WHO THINKS HE CAN!"

Know you can achieve greatness no matter what. It's already in you. Believe you're capable. Believe you can't be stopped. Know you have what it takes to win. The person who believes they can, will! The battle is taking place in your mind!

CHAPTER 8: THE BOOK OF JAMES

I read the Bible a lot, obviously. It's just a really interesting book.

I've read plenty of books within the Bible too. Books like Proverbs, Corinthians 1 & 2, Hebrews, Psalms…so on and so forth.

Proverbs is one of my all-time favorites. It's the reason I decided to start off almost each chapter with a scripture. That book is amazing!

Here's the point: one day, I came across the book of James. I began reading it and was absolutely blown away. I mean, easily one of the best books I've read in the Bible. The author's writing is flawless and his wisdom is on another level.

Topics like going through tough times, how you shouldn't judge your brother, personal favoritism, how faith without works is dead — just a boatload of things. My mind was at capacity after reading it.

Blown away!

That's not even the point. I'm about to hit you with that now.

James 3 talks about "The Untamable Tongue." When I came across that title, I almost passed out. I thought to myself, "Perfect!" So guess what, I'm going to dedicate this chapter to James 3:5-12.

Trust me, it's going to boggle your mind.

Before I start, I want you to read the seven verses below. Take as long as you want. Read them twice if you need to!

James 3:5-12…

> **"5 Likewise, the tongue is a small part of the body, but it makes great boasts. Consider what a great forest is set on fire by a small spark.**

6 The tongue also is a fire, a world of evil among the parts of the body. It corrupts the whole body, sets the whole course of one's life on fire, and is itself set on fire by hell.

7 All kinds of animals, birds, reptiles and sea creatures are being tamed and have been tamed by mankind,

8 but no human being can tame the tongue. It is a restless evil, full of deadly poison.

9 With the tongue we praise our Lord and Father, and with it we curse human beings, who have been made in God's likeness.

10 Out of the same mouth come praise and cursing. My brothers and sisters, this should not be.

11 Can both fresh water and salt water flow from the same spring? 12 My brothers and sisters, can a fig tree bear olives, or a grapevine bear figs? Neither can a salt spring produce fresh water."

I don't know about you, but that's some powerful stuff right there.

Verse seven pops out first. Your tongue has tamed every animal in the food chain. Every creature of the sea. It has the power to tame everything except for itself!

The tongue is untamable. Free-flowing. Wild. Loose like a wild lion.

Are you carrying a deadly concealed weapon in your mouth? Are you killing people with the words you speak? Do your words shoot harmful bullets or bullets of love, revelation and victory?

Take a minute to think about it.

Let's take a look at verse eight.

The Bible says NO man can tame the tongue. It says the tongue is "restless evil" and "full of deadly poison."

Your words can be as deadly as poison. But they can also heal like medicine. It's our choice. We absolutely have to try our best to turn our tongues from poison to words of healing.

Just think about all of the people committing suicide because of bullying? Even cyber bullying, where you can't even see who's saying such ferocious words. It's just a coward hiding behind a computer.

Words have life!

Think about the affect music lyrics have on its listeners. Think about how motivational speakers can change people's lives.

All of these examples are a testament of how strong and powerful the tongue is.

We're all created in the image of God. Not only that, all of us come from Him. He created our bodies. He knows us like the back of His hand (if there is such a thing? ha-ha.)

The Bible says, 7 *"Indeed, the very hairs of your head are all numbered. Don't be afraid; you are worth more than many sparrows." Luke 12:7*

Do you understand how valuable you are to your creator? He loves you so much that He knows the exact amount of hairs on your head.

Unbelievable!

He wants us to use our tongues for edification. To heal. Encourage. Uplift. To represent Him.

Let's go to verse nine.

We praise God but curse our fellow brothers and sisters. We curse them with the same tongue we praise God with. Why not spread love? Why are we so quick to allow our tongues to speak such horrible things about one another? To defile and degrade? To cast judgement? To find fault?

Why?

Why is it easier to tell someone you can't stand them rather than I love you and I care about you?

And we're all of victim of it. Some more than others. I can tell you many stories of how I used to talk about certain people when I was younger. You wouldn't believe it.

But maybe that's a conversation for another time.

Last, but certainly not least, verses 10 through 12.

Just like life and death is in the power of the tongue, so are blessings and curses. Our tongues can be like double-edged swords. The words we use can either cut deep or help people move closer to their destiny. It's our choice. Unfortunately, many of us make the wrong choice. We use our words so poorly.

It shouldn't be that way according to the verse. It doesn't make sense to be that way. We should only be speaking blessings and positivity out of our mouths. Nothing else.

Verse 11 and 12 goes on to explain why.

These verses use water springs and a fig tree as a metaphor to get its point across.

Does it make sense for a water spring to produce fresh water and bitter water at the same time?

No!

No person will drink from it. It'll turn people off. The bitter taste would be disgusting. As it says in the last sentence, *"neither can a salt spring produce fresh water."*

It's either one way or the other. No back and forth. Just flat-out good, refreshing spring water.

The same goes for a fig tree.

It makes no sense for a fig tree to produce olives or a grapevine to produce figs. That's not what makes the tree special. If it were able to do so, it won't help the tree, it'll most likely hinder it simply because it's not meant to produce both.

My friends, use your tongue for one use only — to spread love, not hate. Uplift, not tear down. Speak prosperity. Abundance. Life!

That's what it's meant for. It shouldn't be out of control. Do not let your tongue become a deadly weapon!

CHAPTER 9: SPEAK COURAGEOUS THINGS

6 *"Be strong and courageous, because you will lead these people to inherit the land I swore to their ancestors to give them.* 7 *Be strong and very courageous. Be careful to obey all the law my servant Moses gave you; do not turn from it to the right or to the left, that you may be successful wherever you go." Joshua 1:6-7*

The word courageous was used twice in this verse. That alone defines its importance.

Let's face it. Life is hard. At times, it's a roller coaster ride, scarier than the Dragster at Cedar Point in Sandusky, Ohio.

Truth is, life was never meant to be a cake walk. The struggles of life tend to separate the men from the boys and the women from the girls.

It takes courage to live life. It takes courage to play the cards you were dealt and then persevere.

Adversity will always come. But it hasn't come to stay; it has come to pass. Adversity, setbacks, failures, losses; it has all come to build our character and test our FAITH.

Anyone can be faithful when times are going good. When the dogs are barking, birds are chirping, cats are meowing, money is on point, health is good…you wouldn't need faith.

What about when you've hit a rough season in your life? When storms are kicking your butt like Bruce Lee? The company downsized and you were laid off? When you're struggling in your finances. Life is just coming at you from all angles.

Will you stay focused? Or will you give up?

You have to be courageous. Strong. Tenacious!

Complacency is a no-no. Next thing you know, you look up and you've been stuck for 10 years. Then 10 years turns into 20 years.

Don't get stuck!

I've learned and am still learning that you can't be surprised by the storms you face in different seasons of your life. It's just a small piece of the puzzle to a bigger picture.

In fact, there's a verse that talks about it.

12 *"Dear friends, do not be surprised at the fiery ordeal that has come on you to test you, as though something strange were happening to you." 1 Peter 4:12*

There's a scripture that says — not verbatim — but to this affect: you should feel joy when you face storms.

Most people would say: "Montezz, why should I feel joy when I'm going through a rough period in my life? That makes no sense. I don't want to be unemployed. I don't want to struggle in my finances. I don't want to face opposition. I don't want to be stressed out!"

Trust me, I was just like you when I read that verse. I said, "Huh?" The first thought that came to my head was why in the world would I feel joy when my faith is being tested? When I'm going through a tough time? When I'm broke? When my family isn't close like it should be? My human mind says this makes no damn sense.

Opposition. Trouble. Adversity. Haters. It's all annoying. I don't like it.

None of us do!

Everything you've gone through. Every disappointment. Every setback. Every loss. Every person that has hurt you. It's all apart of the plan from the big man upstairs. I'm not saying He sent those things. I'm simply saying it's NO surprise to Him.

He wants you to dig in your heels and push forward. Everything will start working out for the good. If you give up and get complacent things will stay the same.

In the scripture, many of the people that received their greatest blessing got blessed in times of distress and desperation. They all shared the same thing though. They never gave up because they had the courage to keep going.

In the book of Matthew, Peter walked on water because he had this courage and boldness about him.

While Peter and the other disciples were chilling on the boat in the middle of the sea, Jesus began to appear to them from a distance. He was walking on water. The disciples thought it was a ghost.

They were absolutely terrified. Jesus assured them that he wasn't a ghost.

Peter then developed the courage to ask Jesus if it was really him, command him to step out on the sea. Jesus said "Come." That's all the confirmation Peter needed. He threw up the peace sign to the disciples on the boat, built up the courage, stepped out on faith and walked on water for a little while.

You already know that had to freak the other disciples out. It definitely would've freaked me out.

Just imagine seeing your friend walk on water? Like, what?

It was only when Peter began to doubt that he started to sink. He eventually talked himself out of what he was already doing. His mind couldn't wrap its head around what his body was doing in the spirit. When the mind couldn't conceive it, negative thinking began to creep in and Peter began to panic.

Peter then began to sink, but Jesus grabbed him by the hand and saved him.

That's what doubt does. It can stop a blessing you're already operating in.

There's another example of this in the book of Matthew.

Jesus was headed to heal someone's dead child. A woman who had been suffering from, what the Bible calls, "a flow of blood for twelve years," simply wanted to make contact with Jesus.
In the midst of the crowd, because of her courageousness, the woman managed to touch the hem of his garment and was instantly healed.

For 12 years she couldn't stop bleeding and was called unclean because of it. But with her back against the wall — with all of her might — she saw a healer walking by and did whatever it took to step out on faith and simply touch the hem of his garment. She was healed within a blink of an eye.

Lastly, in the book of Exodus, one of the most famous miracles took place — Moses splitting the Red Sea.

Moses and the people he was delivering out of Egypt were being chased by Pharaoh's finest warriors.

With his back against the wall, Moses stretched out his rod and parted the RED SEA!

How unbelievable is that?

Remember this: GREATNESS is produced from adversity. Opposition makes you go harder. It gives you courage and motivation to persevere no matter what. That's why I truly believe people who have come from nothing end up being successful.

Those who had to fight for it. Struggle for it. Scratch and claw for it. Mother was working three jobs just to pay the bills.

All of it helps build character. Strength. Courage. Tough skin.

James 1:2-4 says 2 ***"Consider it pure joy, my brothers and sisters, whenever you face trials of many kinds,*** 3 ***because you know that the testing of your faith produces perseverance.*** 4 ***Let perseverance finish its work so that you may be mature and complete, not lacking anything."***

You have to be courageous and PATIENT. You've also got to have some dog inside of you. You need to have a never-say-die attitude to chase your dreams.

I want you all to speak courage in all that you do.

You just got a new job. You feel unqualified. It seems like you're in over your head. Negative thoughts start to creep in, telling you *how you can't do the job. What did you get yourself into? You're not qualified.*

Don't listen. Shake it off. Remember, thoughts become things. Whatever you constantly think about in your mind will eventually pop up in reality.

Shake it off.

Be of good courage. Speak courageous things to yourself and the situation. Say, "I can do this. I got this job for a reason. There's nothing too hard for me. I'm more than capable of doing this!"

Build yourself up.

Sometimes the only good things you'll hear said to you are what you say to you!

If you need other folk's compliments to boost your confidence, you've already lost. You'll never be confident or secure within yourself. You'll always be seeking the validation of others.

A famous radio anchor once told me, "Sometimes Montezz, you have to encourage yourself. Don't depend on anyone to do that." Confidence comes from God and it starts from within.

You can't depend on people to give you a compliment. Better yet, you can't depend on people to give you anything. Compliment yourself. Uplift yourself. Self-love is where everything starts.

Everything flows out of the heart. What's in your heart will manifest into thoughts. These thoughts will convince you to confess with your mouth what you're battling in your heart.

That's when things change. The enemy wants you to discourage yourself. He wants you to lack confidence. Not be sure of yourself.

He wants you to be timid. He doesn't want you to be courageous. Fearless. Willing to fight the good fight and persevere.

Nope.

He wants you to shrink. Run away. Be scared. Insecure.

Take those negative thoughts and tell them to kick rocks!

Anything negative comes from a negative source. A negative source can't be from your creator because He's an all-powerful, knowledgeable, overflowing, positive source.

7 "For the Spirit God gave us does not make us timid, but gives us power, love and self-discipline." 2 Timothy 1:7

Don't listen to what the enemy is saying to you or what people are saying to you. Remember to only meditate on what God says about you.

He wants you to have a sound mind. A peaceful mind. Peace and tranquility is what He wants for you. Nothing else. That's just how He operates. I can't explain it. No one can. His ways aren't our ways. The way He tends to do things go beyond our ways.

He thinks on a level that we as a human race can't comprehend. It's out of this world like E.T.

You want to be a manager, but God wants you to be the owner. You want to write just one book, but God wants you to produce five bestsellers.

God's ways aren't our ways!

His abundance meter is off the chain!

I truly want you all to try your best to be courageous in all you do. Speak courage. Speak triumph. I know some things will be more difficult than others. That's understandable. Take baby steps. Nothing happens overnight. Nothing!

Overnight success will disappear overnight.

In the words of Bishop T.D. Jakes, "The strong hen rules the roost."

It takes courage to pursue your dreams. It takes courage to be successful. It's much easier to be mediocre than it is to be successful.

Mediocrity comes easy!

If you don't want to shake things up, stay on the sidelines! Be normal and fit in just like most people. Dress like them, talk like them, walk like them, act like them and think like them! It takes courage to be a winner. I want you to win! Take your courageousness to another level. Go as far as to speak over everything in your life — even your finances.

CHAPTER 10: UPLIFT YOUR FINANCES

19 "A feast is made for laughter, wine makes life merry, and money is the answer for everything." Ecclesiastes 10:19

There's this perception out there that God thinks money is downright evil. And anyone that has money is evil, too.

That's more false than a guy named Santa Claus sliding down your chimney with a big bag of presents.

Did you know there are over 2,000 scriptures about money in the Bible? In fact, Jesus talked more about money than anything except for the kingdom of God.

Hmmm…I wonder why?

Because he knew its importance.

Jesus, the son of God, who was rich in spirit, knowledge and money — although he didn't look like it — understood how an earthly thing like money could be an answer to everything.

He could relate. He lived it. Saw it. Used it.

Jesus even experienced being betrayed for money. Judas betrayed him for 30 stinking pieces of silver.

If it's a thing money can answer it. If it's not a thing money can't answer it.

Money can't buy love. Money can't buy happiness. That's why we see wealthy folk committing suicide.

Money can't buy your health. There are rich people out here who are sick. All the money in the world can't heal them. I guarantee you most of them would give up their riches in a heartbeat if it could take away their sickness.

Money is a thing. It doesn't heal or satisfy matters of the spirit, love or emotion.

It's a thing! A tool.

Things that money can buy? Let's see...Money can pay for your kid's college tuition. Money can pay off your mortgage.

For those of you who graduated from college, money can pay off the student loans you accumulated. Think about it: thousands of dollars worth of debt just wiped away because of an earthly tool called money.

Money can buy you lots of Gucci bags and Louis Vuitton purses, Armani suits, Tom Ford glasses, etc.

Money can pay for that brand new fully loaded Roll Royce you want.

Ladies, money can get you those red bottoms, Chanel bags, Michele watches, lavish massages and more.

If it's a thing, money can pay for it.

God doesn't have an issue with money. It's only when you begin to LOVE the money. Believe in your money. Idol your money!

Worship the money as if it can do something supernatural. Things like healing your aunt of cancer. Helping your best friend get over alcoholism. Curing someone of HIV.

Money can't solve that.

10 "For the love of money is a root of all kinds of evil. Some people, eager for money, have wandered from the faith and pierced themselves with many griefs." 1 Timothy 6:10

Let's get something straight before I go any further. I'm going to keep it real.

All of us want money. All of us! I know I do.

Money brings security. It brings better options. Better food. Better clothes. A better lifestyle. It can give you the best treatment when you're sick.

People who say they don't want money are very misinformed.

Truth is, we need money to survive in this world. It's a necessity.

That's just how it is.

Would you rather live in overflow or struggle for it?

12 *"Wisdom is a shelter as money is a shelter, but the advantage of knowledge is this: Wisdom preserves those who have it." Ecclesiastes 7:12*

Ladies and gents, Money is a SHELTER! Or in other words, money is a defense! It gives you leverage. It can talk for you when your back is against the wall.

On the contrary, if you're in your right mind you can plainly see how people can fall completely in love with money.

I don't know about you, but even if you don't have a million dollars in your account, just imagining it makes you feel good. Just think about all of the things you can scratch off of your to-pay-off list?

Think about the top one percent in the world — the super wealthy. Not rich, but wealthy. There's a difference.

Imagine having that type of money. Really think about a number. Let's say $1 billion dollars, cash!

You can't sit up here and tell me it wouldn't be difficult trying NOT to fall in love with it. The endless things you could do with all of that money is mind-boggling.

But that's where the enemy begins to creep in like a thief in the night. The Lord understands what falling in love with it can do to you. That's why the scripture says, **"for the love of money is the root of all kinds of evil…"**

When you begin to love money it filters down inside and begins to take root. Think about how important roots are when you're trying to grow a successful plant.

The roots go deep down into the ground. They're the foundation. The source of everything. The roots draw valuable minerals from the soil. It then causes the plant to grow and reach its full potential.

In the same way, the root of your body is your spirit. That love for money can begin to reach the root (your spirit) and birth evil things.

People will do some low down things for money. Some will steal, kill and destroy for it. Play politics at work. Suck up to the boss, but talk about that same boss behind their back in the comfort of their home.

Just think about prostitution. Women are willing to have sex with complete strangers just to make a few hundred dollars.

Strippers — no disrespect to the strippers, but there are men and women who show off their entire body just to make some cash!

There are people out here who are hired to kill— all for money.

That's absolutely insane!

My friends, there's nothing wrong with having money or wanting more of it, just don't let it become your idol.

That's why I want you all to speak life over your finances. I've learned and am still learning at this moment that God usually blesses you when your current situation looks the opposite of your destiny — when all hell is breaking loose.

You're working hard, but not reaping the benefits. Finances are lower than four flats on a Cadillac. Your career is flat. No good breaks. No new doors being opened. Things just aren't going right.

Usually it gets tougher right before the tide turns. The key is to keep the faith. Keep moving forward.

Call things that are NOT as though they already are.

Pull up your bank account, even if it hurts your eyes to look at it. Begin to speak abundance over it. Do it every single day. Understand the benefits of stability. Understand how if used correctly, money can answer all things.

It may not happen overnight, but you'll begin to see a shift happen soon. Money will start coming your way from different angles. Life will get easier for you. Less stressful.

It all starts with your thinking and then what you let out of your mouth. If you think your finances will never grow to a place of abundance, they won't. You'll start believing and confessing with your mouth, putting horrible vibes into the atmosphere.

Don't do it!

Remember: faith is the substance of things not seen. It's the things hoped for.

God never intended on us going through life broke, stressed out and struggling.

No way!

He never promised we won't be free from problems, but He does want us to live in overflow.

Here's the key: we have to receive it. We have to believe that we can live that life. If you don't believe it, you'll never receive it. And if you don't receive it, you won't reap the benefits of being financially stable.

Believe it!

Start believing it!

I want you to think about something. Money doesn't transform you into another person. It only enhances the person you truly are. Excuse my language; If you were a butthole before you got money, most likely, you'll be even more of a butthole when you get it.

If you were a nice dresser before you got money, chances are you'll be an even better dresser when you get it.

STAY. THE. SAME!

Be true to yourself.

I don't mean to beat the same drum, but continue to call things that are not as they though they already are!

Believe your finances will grow. Believe you deserve an abundant life. Stand on God's promises. He wants you to live in overflow. He wants you to provide for your family. He wants you to send all of your kids off to college!

College is a HUGE investment. Some colleges cost more than five-bedroom houses.

But that's neither here nor there.

Many people don't receive their blessing because they give up when the breakthrough is right around the corner. It's not going to happen overnight.

When I was trying to land my first TV job as a Sports Anchor/Reporter, it took forever. I filled out hundreds of applications. I sent out hundreds of demo reels. People told me horror stories about how long it took them to get that first gig. And then they gave up.

Not me.

I'm not going to sit up here and tell you I never thought about giving up. I did. Thoughts were telling me to pursue something else. Stray away from the business. Here's the big one: the reason why I hadn't landed a job yet was because I wasn't good enough. That's what the enemy was telling me in my head.

Some days I believed those thoughts. It was a battle. Sometimes you lose battles.

Muhammed Ali lost to Joe Frazier.

The key is to hang in there and win the war!

The breakthrough finally came when I least expected it.

I've said all of that to say, HANG IN THERE. Fight! Tooth and nail. You never know when what you're believing for is going to happen.

You never know when you're going to meet the person of your dreams or get that one call that will propel you to another level.

You never know when that one idea will launch your finances into another dimension.

You just never know!

What you have to do is make sure you're ready to receive it. Make sure you've been preparing for the breakthrough you're believing for. It's better to not have an opportunity and be prepared than to have an opportunity and not be prepared.

Can you handle an abundant increase in your bank account? What do you plan on doing with the money? Will you blow it like making it rain in the strip club?

If you're prepared for the blessing remember to remain true to yourself.

And if you have kids, don't forget about them.

CHAPTER 11: SPEAK POSITIVE WORDS OVER YOUR CHILDREN

6 *"Start children off on the way they should go, and even when they are old they will not turn from it." Proverbs 22:6*

Children are precious. They're a gift from God; the same God that uses a woman's womb as a vessel to birth the child. Children don't come from your mother though. No. They come from God and then through your mother.

How genius is that?

Children are the future. Their innocence and child-like faith is what makes them special. Their brains are like sponges when they're young and developing. That's why it's necessary for you to watch what you speak over their lives when you're raising them.

Train them in the way they should go.

Don't forget our words have power. They manifest into things. Children take heed to what you tell them. They take everything to heart.

There are some grown folk to this day who are battling things that were spoken over their lives as a kid. Some of them are even seeing psychiatrists for it.

That's crazy!

Watch what you say to your kids, as well as what you say around your kids.

They're listening!

I truly believe the process should start early.

Fellas, when your lovely lady is pregnant, talk to the child in her stomach. Speak life while rubbing her beautiful belly. Tell the child how special (s)he is and how (s)he's going to do great things when (s)he gets into the world.

Play good, soothing music. Play tapes that send out positive messages.

After a certain point when the baby is developing in the mother's womb, it can hear things. Why not be proactive in only exposing the kid to positive messages? That includes the words that come out of your mouth.

Positive overcomes negative any day. Feed the child's spirit with faith and life, early!

Tell the child they have a great destiny. Their future is bright. They can do all things through Christ who gives them strength.

Don't stop there. That's only the beginning. You have to continue the process once the child is born. That's when the real work truly begins.

Training up a child is a life-long process. From the time the kid is born to adulthood; as a parent, you're always training the child.

Think of training a child as a seed. Not a job. Everything starts with a seed. And I do mean everything!

You plant the seed by speaking favor, life, faith and positivity into the child when they're young. That seed will eventually sprout and grow, no matter if the child strays away from it. They'll always come back.

Train your child in the way they should go!

Teach them life lessons. Profess they can accomplish all of their dreams if they work hard and smart. Tell them anything is possible. But of course, it takes perseverance, consistency and discipline.

Children are sensitive to things like that. They want the approval of you, the parent. It motivates them. It gives them confidence. Your approval makes them believe they can take over the world.

On the other hand, just as a seed can be planted in a positive environment, it can also be planted in a negative environment — that's where it can potentially produce harsh, toxic fruit.

If you constantly tell your children the total opposite — they don't have what it takes to be successful, they'll never make an impact on the world, they're too small, too short, unattractive, unintelligent, etc., it can possibly limit what they can do in their life.

It's already bad enough when the world doesn't believe in you. But, when your own parents don't approve of you, it really pierces your core.

Parents, don't allow this to happen. Only speak righteous things into the spirit of your kids.

Anything less will limit what they can do in their lives. It'll create a stronghold in their mind that will be very difficult to break.

Remember, it took a while for even the great Les Brown to overcome the stronghold placed in his mind by people when he was a child.

The mind is strong. It's the most important tool we have as humans. Once it gets corrupted, it's extremely difficult to reverse the negativity that has been planted.

Plant nothing but love and prosperity into your children.

Understand they're young, innocent and are sponges! They love you. They look up to you. You're their comforter. You're their problem solver. They come to mommy and daddy because they're under the belief you have all of the answers in the world.

Of course this isn't true, but it's true to them!

You may not be the smartest parent in the world, no parent is, but you can give your child something at a young age that will stick with them forever.

Unique lessons like: having morals, respecting elders, believing in themselves, valuing their education…and on and on.

You do that and I declare your kids will prosper. Everything they touch will succeed. They'll live in abundance to a point where they'll be able to help not only the entire family, but other families as well.

I declare abundance in their health, career, relationships, education and happiness!

Support them in all they do, only if it's legal, of course. Give them great advice and constructive criticism. That's important too.

Do not be a dream killer. If they're not following the crowd, realize that. Don't put them into a box.

Train them in the way they should go!

CHAPTER 12: MEN, CHERISH YOUR WIVES

22 *"He who finds a wife finds what is good and receives favor from the LORD." Proverbs 18:22*

Women are absolutely amazing. God created plenty of great things, but in my opinion, women are up there with air and sliced bread.

There's nothing like a bonafide fine woman, especially if she has her head on straight. A woman with morals, dreams, goals and aspirations is the sexiest thing in the world.

A woman comes from man, thus the name wo-MAN. Fellas, they're our rib, literally. Our backbone too!

Women are nurturers. They're comforters. They soothe us with their beautiful voices while breaking down our barriers of pride in the process. Women are one of God's greatest creations. Brilliant! like the Guinness beer commercial.

None of us would be here if it weren't for a woman. They gave birth to all of us. Everything about women is outstanding.

They're wired completely different from men. They think differently, feel differently and even love differently.

Their bodies are worlds apart from that of a man's. The fact that they can carry a human being inside of them for nine months shows just how unique and special they are.

Our creator purposely didn't design men to give birth to a child. In fact, there's not one hole on a man's body that can produce a child. Matter of fact, I don't even want to think about that right now.

Let's move on.

God knew men wouldn't be able to handle the pain, stress and patience of carrying and giving birth to a child.

Women are naturally built for it.

A woman's body shifts when the baby is developing in the stomach. Their bodies go through mind-blowing changes. Men will never understand.

This is why women should be praised.

This is also why the scripture says, *"Husbands, love your wives..."*

Men, appreciate your wife. Tell her that you love her every day. She's the mother of your kids. She's your queen.

Remember, you chose her, not the other way around. Out of all the beautiful women in the world you felt she was suitable for you! You knew she could be the potential mother of your kids, your sidekick, your go-to guy, so to speak.

That says a lot!

1 Corinthians 11:8-12 really puts into perspective the connection between a man and woman.

Here it is:

8 "For man did not come from woman, but woman from man; 9 neither was man created for woman, but woman for man.

10 It is for this reason that a woman ought to have authority over her own head, because of the angels.

11 Nevertheless, in the Lord woman is not independent of man, nor is man independent of woman.

12 For as woman came from man, so also man is born of woman. But everything comes from God."

The first time I read these scriptures they gave me chills down my spine. Hopefully they really hit home with you too.

Ladies...men...we are meant for one another. Together we can take over the world. Man shouldn't be independent from woman, nor woman from man. When the two are intertwined with love, not only for one another but for God too, it's a beautiful thing.

When women say they don't need a man, that's a lie. When men say they don't need a woman, that's a lie too. The truth is we need each other. We're not meant to be alone.

That's why it's key for each sex to have nothing but the utmost respect for one another no matter the situation. Be careful what you say to your spouse. Marriage is sacred. Marriage is unconditional. Most of all, marriage is a commitment. You can't just leave when you get into an argument or when the storms of life come. The both of you are in it for the long haul!

I understand we're all human and tend to say things that have steep consequences and repercussions, especially when we're operating out of our emotions.

Try not to say things that could potentially ruin the relationship. Instead, when you're feeling the urge to say hurtful things, gather yourself, take a deep breath and walk away. Calm down. Gather your thoughts. Really sit down and blow off some steam.

Take however much time you think you need. When you're done, come back and both of you address the situation. Communicate. Actually listen to what each side has to say. Don't scream or holler because strife only begets more strife.

That's why it's imperative the husband and wife keep their composure when the storms of life come knocking.

Nobody likes storms. They're uncomfortable and stressful. But you can't avoid them. The Bible says rain falls on the just and unjust. Translation: everybody gets it no matter what. You can be the most spiritual person in the entire world. You can pray until your face lights up like a Christmas tree. It still doesn't matter. Rain still falls on the just and unjust.

Fiery trials in a marriage will come. It's inevitable. There's no way around it. But that's why marriage is a union, a partnership — a committed relationship.

When the marriage is in the middle of a storm, that's a time where both of you have to lift one another up! You will be tempted to turn against each other. That's nothing but the enemy trying to cause a division. The enemy is the father of all lies. His only goal is to kill, steal and destroy.

News flash: don't let him!

Stay strong. Stay faithful. Communicate.

Lean on each other for support and remember to pray about the storm the two of you are in. Have faith that God will bring the both of you out better off than you were before.

He wouldn't have allowed it if He wasn't going to turn it around and use it for good. I know it may not seem that way, but it's the truth!

The journey through the storm shapes both of you. The tenacity, perseverance and unwillingness to give up will help lift you through it. The key is to love one another through the process. When your husband is down, lift him up. Men, when your wife is down, lift her up. Be her KING because she's your QUEEN.

Declare you will get through it. Declare no matter what you'll never lose faith. Declare you have the right spouse by your side to be a lifter of your head.

I once heard a pastor say, "A husband and wife must function like two wings on the same bird. They must work together or the marriage will never get off the ground."

Married couples, please work together. Fight the good fight of faith. Fight for your marriage. Fight for longevity. Fight for love.

Keep your marriage off the ground! Husbands, cherish your wives.

CHAPTER 13: WIVES, RESPECT YOUR HUSBANDS

1 "Wives, in the same way submit yourselves to your own husbands so that, if any of them do not believe the word, they may be won over without words by the behaviors of their wives, 2 when they see the purity and reverence of your lives." 1 Peter 3:1-2

I thought it would be fitting to transition from husbands cherishing their wives, to how wives should respect their husbands.

We're living in a world where the divorce rate is at an all-time high. Marriages are torn apart because of money. Men are against women and women against men. I think it's necessary we start making a conscience effort to stop this God-forsaken epidemic.

Ladies, men are simple, and I don't mean that in a bad way. Whether you think so or not, we're intelligent, hard-working and are willing to meet your every need when we're madly in love with you.

Yeah, that's right. We actually do have feelings contrary to popular belief. I know it may not seem that way, but it's the truth. Many of us put up this barrier and conform to how the world thinks a man should think or act from an emotional standpoint. We try to stand strong and hide our feelings because many of us believe it makes us less of a man when we put them on display. That's why men hide their tears in front of you. Some of us don't want to show our vulnerability.

We're natural problem-solvers and providers. It's just in our DNA. When you come to us with an issue our natural instinct is to automatically try to solve it — something like a complicated math problem.

You know what though?

We need your support first. It means so much to us. Your support and encouragement gives us confidence. It gives us courage and strength. It helps us want to go out and "bring home the bacon," so to speak. It makes us want to give you the best possible life.

That said, wives, please respect your husbands. Any opportunity you get to send words of love and favor his way, please do it! They need it. They want it. They cherish it.

Although the Bible says men are the head of the household, you, the wife, help keep the household together. You give it comfort. You make it a home.

Men may be the head, but women are the neck that holds the head in place.

No neck. No head. That's very important.

Team work makes the dream work.

There's already so much pressure to be a man as it is. We're pressured into being financially fit. Provide for the family. There are pressures of becoming successful in all areas of our lives. When a man falls short he doesn't feel like a man. Sometimes he feels less than.

Wives, make an effort to relieve that pressure.

Make things easier for him. Encourage him. Lift his spirits after a long day of work. Tell him you need him and that you're his back-bone. Your words are so valuable to him. The both of you are one flesh.

Act like it!

As a matter of fact, the scripture puts it this way: 24 *"That is why a man leaves his father and mother and is united to his wife, and they become one flesh." Genesis 2:24*

A man will leave his own mother and father — the people who raised him, clothed him, fed him — just to find you. You, his wife, his queen. The mother of his future kids.

The scripture says, "one flesh." One being. One spiritual connection is the result of marriage. If this is true, then the frequency at which the wife and husband should be vibrating on needs to be inseparable, unbreakable and unshakable.

That means no matter what the both of you go through make sure to be there for one another. Lift each other's head in times of need. Communicate instead of isolating yourselves. When trouble comes — and it will — that's when, more than ever, the two of you should come together to figure things out.

James 5:16 says, 16 *"Therefore confess your sins to each other and pray for each other so that you may be healed. The prayer of a righteous person is powerful and effective."*

Love unconditionally.

The two of you made an agreement before God. The creator of the universe. The God who spoke worlds into existence. Flung stars into space. Created the heavens and the earth.

Wives love your husbands. He may not be the most successful guy in the world. He may not even have the most money, the best job, etc. But, my challenge to you is to continue to lift his spirits. Your encouraging, nurturing words are more valuable than you can even begin to imagine.

If he's trying his best. Working hard. Grinding to make a better life. Keep encouraging him.

I get sick and tired of hearing the verbal abuse many wives send in the direction of their husbands. It goes both ways, but since this chapter is about wives respecting husbands, I'm just going to stay on topic.

When will you understand men don't respond well to constant criticism all day, every day? A man wants to hear, especially from his woman, "Baby, I'm so proud of you. You're the best husband in the world. You're so strong. So handsome. I'm happy to be married to you."

They don't want to hear this: "You ain't nothing. Why aren't you as successful as him? Why can't you do this? Why aren't you doing that?"

That will turn a man completely off!

Eventually he'll start to look for a woman that's nicer and compliments him even when he doesn't deserve it. I'm not saying I condone this behavior because I don't. I'll never agree with cheating or divorce.

What I'm saying is that there will come a time when a man will get sick and tired of not hearing anything encouraging or uplifting come out of your mouth.

Train your tongue!

When love and encouragement flows out of your mouth, your husband will automatically gain more strength and confidence. He'll be more motivated to do whatever it takes to make you happy.

Words cut deep. You should know that by now just from reading this book. Words manifest and take root.

As a wife, if you're throwing sharp daggers at your husband in the form of words, what are you doing?

Not only should your actions show him your unconditional, unwavering love — your words should too! And again, this goes both ways. I'm just simply staying on topic.

If you have a good husband, a good man, a man with morals, a man with a sense of purpose, a man who's trying his best to create the best possible life for himself, his wife and kids, please — I repeat — please, respect that.

So what he isn't a millionaire. So what he isn't driving a Bentley. So what he isn't some CEO of a Fortune 500 company. Love him for who he is, as well as for who he isn't.

After all, that's what makes him special.

Wives, respect your husbands. He's trying his best.

This is why I love the relationship Bishop T.D. Jakes has with his wife, Serita Jakes. They've been married for over 30 years, but it wasn't always peaches and cream. Jakes will tell you himself that they've been through the good, bad, ugly and butt ugly.

Their partnership is strong. And it only got that way because of the hard times they faced together. Instead of giving up on each other they rode it out.

He and his wife married in 1981. He was a young, up-and-coming pastor who was struggling to make ends meet.

To make things worse, just six months into their marriage, Bishop Jakes and Serita survived a horrible car crash that left Serita with severe leg and foot injuries. Many doctors said Serita would never walk again.

Times were rough.

Bishop Jakes thought to himself, "The Devil is a lie!"

He stood by her side. He prayed for her, clothed her, cooked for her, washed her hair and even taught her how to walk again.

Jakes spoke nothing but victory over her during what was probably the worst time of her life. He would consistently tell her, "You can do this," while he'd be teaching her how to walk. Eventually Serita made a full recovery.

I can only imagine how difficult it was, but they made it through. Their bond grew stronger because of it. They grew stronger in love and in faith.

What was Bishop Jakes doing? Standing by her side. Using his actions and words to show how much he loved her. She's his queen, his wife. It was his responsibility.

Serita returned the favor when Jakes had fallen on hard times and was struggling in his finances. At one point in his life he almost lost everything. He lost his car. His lost his friends. He lost his credit. There were times where he struggled to feed himself because he couldn't afford groceries. And the big one — he even lost confidence in himself.

Through that entire period, Serita stood by his side. She continued to support him. She continued to believe in him. She continued to stand strong by his side because that's what a great wife is supposed to do.

She didn't want to leave him because he was broke. She valued him entirely too much. Serita understood he wasn't always going to be that way. I can imagine her speaking life into him, lifting his spirits. Lifting his head.

I've seen and heard hundreds of disaster stories where a wife would look down on her husband because he was struggling in his finances. All kinds of negativity coming out of her mouth, like how he's a failure, a joke, or how she wished she would've married a more successful man — a man more accomplished.

No!

Don't be that way. Work with your man. He's only human. Yes, the man should be able to stand strong, but there will be times where you'll have to be his strength. A person can only handle so much. Sometimes he just wants to hear these four words: "Baby, I got you." That's all. Those simple four words can light a fire under him.

Do you know how many women today will flat-out leave their man just because he's struggling at one point in his life? That's awful. Terrible, and any other negative word you want to label it.

News flash!

You're highly misinformed if you believe you're not going to have to struggle at some point in your life. Everything won't be peaches and cream.

Everything's not going to go right 100 percent of the time. That's not how things work. That Bible warns us of this in plenty of scriptures.

If a wife is willing to bail on her husband just because he's struggling she wasn't his wife to begin with.

Point blank period.

You stick around through thick and thin, and in that process, you are to be as encouraging and uplifting as humanly possible.

Never kick a person while they're already down. That's weak. Your true character is being brought to the forefront.

There was another incident in Bishop Jakes' life where his wife was extremely supportive at a time when he most needed it. He was living in West Virginia, working as a pastor. He needed a church badly. I mean, really needed it. He went into bank, after bank, after bank, hoping to get a loan for a new church building.

Four banks rejected him.

We all know that there's nothing like rejection when you truly need something.

After the fifth bank turned him down he pulled up to his house and stayed in the driveway so Serita wouldn't see him. He had just got the call saying the loan didn't go through. He sat in the car crying. Not only was getting this loan a necessity, it came at a time where Bishop Jakes was unsure of himself as a man and as a leader.

To add insult to injury, he was already battling something that was tormenting him mentally — the spirit of thinking he wasn't good enough.

And then here comes his lovely wife to uplift his spirit, to nurture him. Using her words to heal her husband's pain — standing by his side, I can imagine Serita saying "Baby, everything will be fine. It doesn't matter. We'll get there. We'll do whatever we got to do."

She spoke words that were sweet to his soul and healthy to his bones.

How beautiful is that? Unconditional love.

I've said all of this to say, wives, please love, respect and cherish your husbands. Even in tough times. Don't give up. He needs you! He needs your support. He needs you to be his rib.

Despite the trepidation, be that rib he so desperately needs.

And for the married millennials, have patience with one another.

You're going to be growing together for the rest of your lives. You're going to change as the years go by. Accept the challenges that come with change. Communicate with one another. Grow together. Your bond will be unbreakable.

CHAPTER 14: MILLENNIALS

18 "But the things that come out of a person's mouth come from the heart, and these defile them." Matthew 15:18

Of course I had to write a chapter about millennials. I'm one of them. I was born on Jan. 16, 1988.

Many millennials get a bad rap. A lot of the older generation tend to think we're lazy, prideful, arrogant young thunder cats who have no idea what we're doing in life. Others may believe we're spoiled no-it-alls who don't want to put in the work to become successful. We were taught to believe we can have what we want and become anything we want in this life.

Anything!

Some believe we want to take the easy route to success. We want to sit on our young asses and create ways for easy wealth and then reap all of the benefits of success without going through the struggle.

Let me be the first to say this couldn't be any further from the truth.

To be fair, of course there are those out there who have no vision, goals or aspirations, but they aren't just millennials. You can find a 50-year-old man or woman who has nothing better to do than play career mode on a video game.

Age has nothing to do with it.

Whether you like it or not, millennials are the future. And the future's looking bright.

I want the older generation to understand that the vast majority of us aren't arrogant know-it-alls. Many of us value the counsel of the past generation because they've been there and done that. The older generation is wiser. They have more understanding.

12 "Is not wisdom found among the aged? Does not long life bring understanding?" Job 12:12

Millennials, the opportunities you have in front of you are endless. The digital age has opened up so many doors. We're technologically savvy guru's in social media and well-versed in an array of areas.

Millennials are even the nation's most educated generation in history when it comes to having college degrees. That's according to an article written on the Pew Research Center's website entitled, *"More Millennials, a Bachelor's Degree Continues to Pay Off, but a Master's Earns Even More."*

Millennials are persistent, passionate and willing to do whatever it takes to reach success. And yes, that means working very hard and embracing the struggle.

But that's not what this chapter is about. Selfishly, I just wanted to get that off of my chest because I represent for my millennials.

Although I love being a millennial, at times I really get disgusted at how we talk to each other —how we speak to one another as well as the older generation for that matter. And for those who have kids, how you speak to them too!

Understand we wouldn't be here if it weren't for the older generation. They paved the way for us. Respect their authority.

Leviticus 19:32 says, 32 "Stand up in the presence of the aged, show respect for the elderly and revere your God. I am the LORD."

My fellow millennials, please respect your elders. Respect those who have come before you.

Hold your tongue. Don't curse them. They're a gift from God. They're there to give you wisdom and to keep you out of harm's way.

I'm not telling you to be naive. I'm talking about the one's with sense.

If you're in a position where you don't have the best relationship with your parents or grandparents, still try your best to hold your tongue. I know it's tough. Especially when they're verbally abusive. There will be times when you just can't handle it anymore and you'll go the heck off!

That's fair.

Look, we're only human beings. At times you'll give in. I'm only saying find ways to shake it off.

The same goes for the elderly. Clearly, there's a gap between millennials and the older generation. Don't abuse the authority that you all have. Respect the opinions of the young gunz. Valuable wisdom doesn't always come out of an elder's mouth.

OK. Back to the point at hand.

My fellow millennials, I get absolutely disgusted at how we act at times. It's almost like who in the world raised you? I'm not saying that to offend your parents, but at some point it's like, my goodness. The way you act and talk is insanely scary.

Try to remember that iron sharpens iron. And whatever you reap, you will most definitely sow.

The more you speak love, the more people will speak love to you. The more you uplift, the more people will uplift you. The same can be said for the complete opposite. You hate, people will hate on you. You treat people with disrespect, people will disrespect you.

Treat others how you want to be treated! The vibes you send off into the universe will come back to you tenfold.

Millennials, we go through so much already: the pressures of being successful, wanting to make it, people believing we feel entitled. On top of that, many of us get frustrated because we're trying to simply find our way in this world.

Let's not make it more difficult on ourselves.

I want you all to do me a favor. Get still. Analyze yourself. Recognize strife only begets more strife. Uplift your fellow millennials. Tell them how important they are and that they're on the way to doing big things in life — things that will change the face of the earth. That's what's important.

As millennials, many of us get caught up in the latest fads, especially in fashion.

For the guys, if you aren't rocking the flyest new kicks, Gucci belt, outfit, driving the best car, have a prestigious job title, etc. we have this tendency to judge and talk about the next man that doesn't have those things, acting as if they're less than.

Let me tell you, possessions don't make a person, the person makes the possessions. If you feel as though you're "the man" just because you have nice shoes, cars, clothes and other worldly things, it's time to grow up!

That reminds me of an interview I came across on YouTube with the great Bob Marley. It was an interview with *60 minutes*.

A reporter asked Marley: "Have you made a lot of money out of your music?"

Marley responded: "Money…how much is a lot of money to you?

Reporter: "That's a good question. Have you made, say, millions of dollars?"

Marley: "Nahh."

Reporter: "Are you a rich man?"

Marley: "When you mean rich, what ya' mean?"

Reporter: "Do you have a lot of possessions? A lot of money in the bank?"

Marley: "Possessions make you rich? I don't have that type of richness. My richness is life, forever."

Marley was saying your possessions mean nothing at the end of the day. The real gift is life and making a strong impact on others while you're here so your legacy will live on forever.

It's not about your belt, your shoes, your clothes, your crib, your looks or your job.

It's about the impact you have on others.

To my beautiful young ladies: don't talk down on your fellow sisters just because she isn't doing as well in life as you are. Just because she doesn't have the flyest Louis Vuitton bag, red bottoms, weave, etc. it doesn't mean she adds no value to life.

You just never know what a person is going through. You never know! One word of encouragement can make someone's day. One word could ultimately launch them into another dimension of their destiny. Always keep that in mind.

Be a lifter of their head when they're down. Build each other up. Bounce ideas off one another. Believe in them as God believes in you.

Only small-minded people are critical, fault-finding and negative. They never want to see you succeed. As long as you're on the same level as them, they're happy. But the minute you want to advance in life they begin to turn on you.

Don't be that person. No matter what, always be a comforter. Speak great words that will manifest and take root. Manage the idol words that are coming out of your mouth.

Millennials, be conscience of how you talk to each other.

Honor one another! Help guide each other toward your purpose instead of destroying it. Whatever you send out into the atmosphere will ultimately come back to you!

I truly believe God put us here to not only find our purpose and then do His will, but to serve others as well. To spread love and not hate.

That reminds me of a time when some friends and I were coming from a restaurant in downtown Chicago. We were headed to another spot to have food and a few drinks. While walking to the bar, we bumped into a guy standing on the street smoking a cigarette. He couldn't have been more than 25-years-old. Obviously that made him a millennial.

One of my friends stopped into a 7-Eleven store to grab a snack. While he was in there I began making small talk with the guy.

Eventually we got on the subject of life and trying to do positive things while we're alive. This dude eventually started spilling his beans. He was in that street life selling drugs and whatnot.

My other friend finally walked out of the 7-Eleven and all of us began to walk and talk. In the middle of the guy speaking to us something began to rise up in my spirit — my friend's spirit too! Both of us had the sudden urge to minister to him.

Finally, when he was done speaking, my friend and I began to speak faith, life and prosperity into his spirit.

We told him he was a young black KING. He was smart, intelligent, handsome and filled with talents that he hadn't even tapped into yet. We didn't stop there. We just kept on going. He had the power to change the world if he was willing to give up the life he was living and head toward a more positive lifestyle.

Our goal was to help him stray away from the path he was currently on because it was only going to lead to destruction.

As we were doing this it was obvious the words we were speaking were having an impact on him.

This went on for at least an hour or so. This fella mentioned how he wanted to get out of the street life, but it was difficult because of the fast money. Even though there was a stronghold on his life, you can tell he wanted to get out of it and pursue something better.

He knew deep down inside he was meant to do better things.

My friend and I didn't know this guy from a grain of salt. We literally just ran into him on the street.

Here's the point…

Do you see how we immediately began to speak great things into his future although we didn't know him? He might not have showed it on the outside, but our words were punching his spirit like Mike Tyson hitting his punching bag.

We gave him lots of encouragement instead of judging him for the current lifestyle he was living.

Imagine if we decided to go the complete opposite way. After hearing the type of lifestyle he was living, what if we started to judge him? Count him out? Tell him he wasn't going to be anything in life?

For one, he might've tried to fight us simply because he was from the hood. That type of disrespect can get you beat down — or even killed.

Two: it wouldn't have done him any justice. Most likely, he would've continued to go down the same path without caring about ending up in jail again or even dead.

After some time had passed, we finally called it quits; we left him and eventually went on to our destination.

We might not ever see him again, but I can guarantee you this: he will never be the same. The words we spoke over him stirred up something. We did our job.

If you have good things in your heart, it's going to flow out like oil and affect everybody you come across.

Let's put it in Bible talk.

45 *"A good man brings good things out of the good stored up in his heart, an evil man brings evil things out of the evil stored up in his heart. For the mouth speaks what the heart is full of." Luke 6:45*

If there's evil stored up in your heart, then it'll eventually flow out like a water fountain. You can't stop it.

Since there's good in my heart, I automatically wanted to speak good things into his life.

Millennials, analyze your hearts. What's inside of it? Do good things flow out of it? Or negativity? If so, what do you need to do in order to change what flows out of it?

Whatever it is, make the change now.

CHAPTER 15: SOW SEEDS WHEREVER YOU GO

9 "Love must be sincere. Hate what is evil; cling to what is good. 10 Be devoted to one another in love. Honor one another above yourselves. 11 Never be lacking zeal, but keep your spiritual fervor, serving the Lord. 12 Be joyful in hope, patient in affliction, faithful in prayer. 13 Share with the Lord's people who are in need. Practice hospitality." Romans 12:9-13

Did you know every time you show honor you're sowing a seed?

We should make an effort to honor someone everywhere we go, whether we know them or not. Find people who you can uplift and encourage — someone you can compliment and make feel better about themselves.

Pour out that oil of honor.

When you do this you're son wing a seed. In turn, the seed you sow will bloom and cause blessings to chase you down. The favor on your life will begin to increase.

Remember this principle: the honor you show others will eventually become a blessing to you. You can't receive nothing you aren't willing to give away first.

This is why in the scripture it says, **35 *"In everything I did, I showed you that by this kind of hard work we must help the weak, remembering the words the Lord Jesus himself said: 'It is more blessed to give than to receive.'" Acts 20:35***

In a world where everyone is busy and things are moving so fast, it can sometimes be tough to find time to honor people. But you have to learn how to make it a priority.

Take time out to tell that coworker how good they're doing on the job; how the company should be proud to have them working there. Make them feel special. It'll go a long way.

When you're eating at a restaurant. Talk to your waiter or waitress. Tell them they're providing excellent service. Tell their supervisor how good of a job they're doing.

Honor them.

That janitor at work, most people look down on janitors. They work long hours cleaning up after people's messes. Their job seems insignificant. Truth is, without the janitor the office would most likely be a pigsty.

Take time out to thank them for what they're doing. Tell them you appreciate how they take pride in cleaning up the office, taking out the trash and vacuuming. A simple thank you can go a long way.

Each and every day we should seek ways to compliment people. Never miss opportunities to be good to someone. That oil of honor, never be stingy with it.

Someone gets a promotion at work. The position they were hired for was the same one you applied to. You really wanted it. Instead of getting upset or jealous, congratulate them. Tell them they deserve it. Encourage them. Tell them how they'll be a great fit for the job and how the company made the right decision.

When you do this you're planting seeds and the roots are going deeper and deeper into the ground. You'll begin to see things shift in your entire life once the plant breaks through the dirt.

I've learned over the years that showing honor to others not only makes them feel special, but it makes you feel good down on the inside too. You'll be surprised how the simplest form of honor can heal.

Joel Osteen said in one of his sermons, "Be generous with your compliments, be stingy with your complaints. Be free with your honor. Withhold the dishonor."

Galatians 6:8-10 puts it this way.

8 "Whoever sows to please their flesh from the flesh will reap destruction; whoever sows to please the Spirit, from the Spirit will reap eternal life. 9 Let us not become weary in doing good, for at the proper time we will reap a harvest if we do not give up. 10 Therefore, as we have opportunity, let us do good to all people, especially to those who belong to the family of believers."

I've seen this in my life as well.

I remember accepting a position at the No. 1 news radio station in Chicago. Not only did it look good on my resume, it was a job full of well-seasoned veterans who've been in the journalism game for over 20 years.

I was so excited when I got the job. I thought to myself, "Did I really just land this gig? Really? Wow! Time to do work!"

Fast forward to my first day on the job. It was a training session. I had many people training me in various shifts, but two really stood out to me.

Let me tell you, I was absolutely overwhelmed by the workload. Oh. My. Goodness!

Now, don't get me wrong, I took great notes. Studied the notes. Tried my best. But those first two or three weeks of training, I was absolutely overwhelmed by how much I had to remember.

I even started to question myself like "Did I even take the right job?"

Yeah. It was that bad.

Fast forward about three or four months later. I became pretty good at the job thanks to the training from two people.

Here's the point: to this day I constantly tell those who trained me, thank you — all the time! Sometimes I take it even further. I'd say how great they are at their job. I'd say things like "You're the man."

I stress that if it weren't for them I wouldn't have gotten good at the job.

That's not something I have to do; it's something I want to do. I'm pouring out honor. Storing up my blessings.

I could've easily gotten the big head and not have thanked them for helping me improve at the job I was hired for. I'd be a fool to think that way.

The scripture says, 3 **"For by the grace given me I say to every one of you: Do not think of yourself more highly than you ought, but rather think of yourself with sober judgment, in accordance with the faith God has distributed to each of you." Romans 12:3**

It was because of their great training that I had gotten pretty good at being an assistant producer. I will never stop thanking them. It's the simple things.

Here's another one.

My mentor, Rob Parker, a true legend in the journalism biz. At a time when I was absolutely discouraged because I couldn't find another job in my field, Rob would constantly pour out his version of oily honor on my head.

Your boy was struggling, y'all. After I was laid-off from a company in 2016, I went on interview, after interview, after interview. I must've sent out over 300 emails to different news directors, hoping that one of them would give me an opportunity to prove myself. I got about three call backs.

Three!

I was struggling in my finances, barely paying my bills. As a matter of fact, my mother was helping me pay my bills. I was struggling in my faith. Struggling with my emotions. My little mind couldn't wrap itself around the fact that I wasn't landing a job. I had the degrees. I had the resume. I had the work ethic. I had the skills. Nothing was happening for me and I really couldn't understand why.

Then I got desperate. I started applying for everything: retail jobs, communications jobs, jobs I wasn't even interested in. I applied for everything but a stripper or escort position. I was low, but not that low.

I remember going on an interview for a company in Evanston, Illinois — a startup. It was for a digital advisor position. When I tell you to this day, I still don't know what the role was, I'm not lying. I was flat-out desperate. I had a great interview. I just knew they were going to hire me. I was wrong. The human resources lady sent me that devastating email the next day.

You know the one.

It went a little something like this: "Thank you so much for taking the time out to speak to our Digital Advisor team this week. After some deliberation, they've decided to not move forward with your candidacy at this time."

I was crushed. I even cried. Honestly, I didn't even want the job like that. I just needed the money. And that's exactly why God didn't open up that door.

At the time, my mother would keep telling me it just wasn't my season. She was absolutely right.

It seemed like every single time I went on social media someone had just landed a job. A great job at that. The spirit of jealousy very rarely dwells inside of me, but my goodness I thought to myself: "Here I am applying my butt off to jobs and can't get one!"

I felt like a low-life. I didn't feel like a man. It was just all-around tough.

Here's the point. No matter what I was going through. No matter how down and out I got. Rob would always tell me to keep my head up. To keep on pushing. That I was talented enough to make it in the biz. I just have to believe in myself because if I don't, no one else will.

He was showing honor, uplifting my spirits, telling me to keep on trying. The honor he continuously showed me helped me get through one of the toughest storms of my life.

Friends, the world is already filled with so much hate, deceit and evil. It's bad enough that many people talk down on one another. They rather discourage than encourage and seek revenge rather than forgiveness.

Don't be like the masses. Be different. Standout. Honor each other. Find ways to make somebody's day. Go out of your way to do it. But only if it's sincere. Anybody can act. Anybody can pretend, but this ain't the Oscars.

Matthew 5:14 says, 5 *"You are the light of the world. A town built on a hill cannot be hidden."* Verse 16 goes on to say, 16 *"In the same way, let your light shine before others, that they may see your good deeds and glorify your Father in heaven."*

Let your light shine within the world. When you honor people you're letting your light shine bright like the stars in space. I challenge you to be a star in a universe full of asteroids and meteorites.

Asteroids and meteorites cause destruction. Stars illuminate.

Which one are you?

Look in the mirror. Analyze yourself. Search your heart. Do you have the urge to honor or do you tend to pass up that opportunity?

CHAPTER 16: HONOR YOUR MOTHER AND FATHER

12 *"Honor your father and your mother, so that you may live long in the land the LORD your God is giving you." Exodus 20:12*

This chapter is an extension of the previous one. I've decided to go a bit deeper about how you should honor one another. I know I've touched on this in previous chapters, but God put it on my heart to expand on this topic. This time it's about your parents.

Friends, if your mother or father or both are in your life, you're blessed. Think about the people who have never met their parents. Think about the kids living in foster homes because their birth parents decided to give them up for adoption. Just think about that.

You're blessed!

Honor your mother and father. You only get one. After they're gone, that's it. You'll never get them back. They put clothes on your back, food in your stomach when you're hungry, gave you shelter and sound advice when you needed it.

Let's take it even further. When you were a baby, they cleaned up after you when you'd use the bathroom on yourself. That's right. That nasty boo-boo and urine. They changed your diaper. I bet some of your parents even got some of it on them. Ugh. If that ain't love, I don't know what is. Name any other person who can boo-boo on you and not get their butt whooped?

Don't worry. I'll wait.

A parent's love is unconditional. Please don't take it for granted.

Use your words to express gratitude. Don't be afraid to tell your parents you love them. Thank them for everything they've done in your life. Thank them for raising you and helping you to become the person you are today.

Take heed to their counsel. You have two ears and one mouth for a reason. You ever wonder why that is?

It's because you're supposed to listen more than you should be talking.

Remember, your parents have been there and done that. They're not here to be your best friend.

No!

They're there to give you guidance, to help you NOT make the same mistakes they made when they were young and spry like you are.

Realize that no matter what you do, no matter how many times you hurt them, deceive them, lie to them, they'll always be in your corner.

Some of you are probably thinking: "Montezz, you don't know my parents. We just don't have the best relationship."

Truly I tell you, I completely understand some of you don't or didn't have the best parental guidance growing up. Or maybe your parents were or are still verbally abusive. I understand because I've been there.

It's hard not reacting to someone who consistently belittles you with their words. Your first instinct is to pop-off at the mouth. But remember this: strife only begets more strife.

Don't, I repeat, don't curse your parents. No matter how mad you get with them. Just. Don't. Do it!

Your words are like sharp daggers. For those who have seen the movie *Kill Bill* — volume one or two — your tongue can be sharp as a Hattori Hanzo sword. I know it's tough, but don't do it. Turn the other cheek.

Whatever your parents do to you, forgive them!

Take Joyce Meyer for example. If you're not familiar with her, she's one of the greatest pastors the world has seen. Look up Joyce Meyer Ministries. She's preached all over the world to thousands and thousands of people.

Do you know she was sexually, mentally, emotionally and verbally abused by her own father when she was young?

Yes. Her own father abused her sexually! On her website — joycemeyer.org — she told how she was raped at least 200 times. Raped at least every week until she was 18-years-old.

Meyer's father was mean, controlling and manipulative for most of his life. Because of that alone, her household was covered with fear because he was so unstable that you'd never know what he was going to do. There was so much tension in her house that she'd dread going home from school.

Where was Meyer's mother in all of this? Well, Meyer said her mother was too cowardly to step up and do something about it. Instead, she just stood idle. Limp. Frozen. She did nothing.

"I guess on some levels, I can understand that. It's much easier to believe your 9-year-old daughter is a liar than it is to believe that the man you married could be capable of something so awful," Meyer said in an article written on charismamag.com.

Meyer also told how she prayed that her father would die, that God would remove her from the situation.

Although God never delivered her from that problem, He did give her the strength to get through it. Now Meyer is living in overflow. God repaid her double for her trouble. He also worked out every-thing for her good.

Here's the point.

Yes, what she went through was absolutely awful. It's probably one of the worst possible situations a young child can go through. I can't even imagine going through something like that.

But you know what, in the end, Meyer ended up forgiving her father. Better yet, while he was in the hospital, she moved her father close to her house and took care of him. She consistently told him she loved him. Every need he had, she met. She fed him. Bought him clothes— the whole nine.

Meyer's father eventually apologized to her. He had been wanting to do it for a long time, but just couldn't bring himself to do it.

What am I saying?

If Meyer can forgive her own father for sexually abusing her as a child, you can forgive your parents for whatever they've done to you.

Whatever division has been caused between you and your parents, hash it out with your words. Call a family meeting. Do whatever it takes to repair the relationship. You'll feel much better that you did. You'll feel a weight come off of you.

Speak nothing but good things about your parents. Again, they're not going to be here forever. Make an attempt to encourage them every day. Tell them you love them and that they're the best parents in the world, even if they're not. It doesn't matter. They're your parents!

Don't be foolish. Try not to do or say things that'll damage your relationship with them.

There are plenty of scriptures that talk about how your foolishness can impact your mother and father.

25 *"A foolish son brings grief to his father and bitterness to the mother who bore him." Proverbs 17:25*

Proverbs 10:1 also says, 1"The proverbs of Solomon: A wise son brings joy to his father, but a foolish son brings grief to his mother."

Friends, the things you do, the things you say, if they're negative, it can have a tremendous impact on both of your parents. "Grief" and "bitterness" are strong words. When a person is battling a lot of grief and bitterness it can make them sick. It can weigh them down. Destroy their spirit. Sometimes it can even cause them to give up on life.

Don't allow this to happen to your parents.

And yes, I know we're all human. As long as we live we're going to hurt the ones we love. That's apart of life. We all make mistakes.

The question is, is your heart in the right place? Are you intentionally being foolish? Do you understand your acts of foolishness are causing your parents to grow weary and bitter? Or is it that you just don't care?

You have to understand it's hard being a parent. But then again, if you're not one — it's hard to comprehend. My mother always tells me, "Montezz, you won't understand until you have kids."

It's a lot of responsibility, so try not to make it harder for them. Give them ease.

Honor your mother and father. They're simply there to guide you. Especially during times of trials and tribulations.

You only get one. I can't stress that enough. Many children would kill to have their parents in their lives. They wish they had a mother to tell them, "I love you," or a father say, "I'm proud of you my son."

But the good news is that God will be a mother to the motherless and a father to the fatherless.

Friends, honor your mother and father so all will be well with you!

CHAPTER 17: SPEAK TRIUMPH IN THE MIDDLE OF THE TRIAL

6 *"In all this you greatly rejoice, though now for a little while you may have had to suffer grief in all kinds of trials. 7 These have come so that the proven genuineness of your faith — of greater worth than gold, which perishes even though refined by fire — may result in praise, glory and honor when Jesus Christ is revealed." 1 Peter 1:6-7*

I've touched on trials in multiple chapters of this book, but now I feel the need to write an entire chapter on it.

Truth is, I don't know one person who likes going through tough times, storms, trials or whatever you want to call them.

Not one!

At some point in our lives, we'll all have to face trials and tribulations. Whether it's financially, in our health, on the job, in our family, etc.

They're stressful, very uncomfortable and many times they make no sense. What makes it worse is that we can't see them coming. Only one person can: God!

God knew before any of us showed up on this planet that we'll go through many trials and afflictions. That's why He warned us about them in plenty of scriptures.

Here's one from the book of James.

12 **"Blessed is the one who perseveres under trial because, having stood the test, that person will receive the crown of life that the Lord has promised to those who love him."** **James 1:12**

And in case you forgot, here's another one from the book of Peter that I've mentioned before.

12 "Dear friends, do not be surprised at the fiery ordeal that has come on you to test you, as though something strange were happening to you. 13 But rejoice inasmuch as you participate in the sufferings of Christ, so that you may be overjoyed when his glory is revealed." 1 Peter 4:12-13

Peep what Jesus said to his disciples in Luke 22:28: 28 *"You are those who have stood by me in my trials."*

Checkout this scripture from Deuteronomy.

19 "You saw with your own eyes the great trials, the signs and wonders, the mighty hand and outstretched arm, with which the Lord your God brought you out. The Lord your God will do the same to all the peoples you now fear." Deuteronomy 7:19

One more.

29 "For it has been granted to you on behalf of Christ not only to believe in him, but also to suffer for him, 30 since you are going through the same struggle you saw I had, and now hear that I still have." Philippians 1: 29-30

God warned us in so many ways so we wouldn't think something strange is happening to us, something we didn't deserve, something that wasn't just or unfair. Fact is, the same God that orders our steps into victory can also order our steps into a storm.

You're probably thinking, "Montezz, if God is so good, why would He allow me to go through this sickness? This financial difficulty? I need my health. I need to pay my bills. Why? Why? Why?"

Truth is, I don't have the answer to that. God is omnipotent. Sovereign. He's known as the great "I AM." His ways of thinking are above our ways. He's a complete mystery.

1 Corinthians 2:7-9 puts it this way:

7 "No, we declare God's wisdom, a mystery that has been hidden and that God destined for our glory before time began. 8 None of the rulers of this age understood it, for if they had it, they would not have crucified the Lord of glory. 9 However, as it is written:

"What no eye has seen, what no human mind has conceived — the things God has prepared for those who love him..."

Verse 11 goes on to say, 11 *"For who knows a person's thoughts except their own spirit within them? In the same way no one knows the thoughts of God except the Spirit of God."*

Brothers and sisters, whatever storm you're going through or will eventually go through, God is in control of it. He controls the heat. He would've never allowed it if He wasn't going to turn it around and use it for your good. He would've never allowed it if it were going to stop you from reaching your destiny.

Period!

Here's the key: **YOU. HAVE. TO. STAY. IN. FAITH!**

Believe it's going to get better. Believe things will turn around. Believe He's going to use it for your good.

Many people fall apart when trials come. They get bitter. They complain, saying, "God, why is this happening to me?"

Sometimes they'll even give up on life because their mind has convinced them the storm will last forever.

The enemy gives you an allusion that things will never change. An illusion like a thirsty man in the desert looking at a mirage of a water spring. If you let that negative thought take root, next thing you know you'll believe. Once you believe it you'll start to get stuck. And when you get complacent — it's all downhill from there.

Many times people develop this victim mentality instead of a VICTOR mentality.

My friends, nothing lasts forever. However, if you give up, it will! Seasons change. Summer never lasts forever. Winter never lasts forever. Spring never lasts forever. Fall never lasts forever.

Seasons change! There's always sunshine after the storm.

The enemy gives you this perception that it'll never get better. It's going to be like that until the very day you die.

Don't believe those thoughts!

Jesus told a parable in the book of Matthew that really puts things into perspective.

There were two men building new houses. One built his house on a rock. The other built his house on sand.

Eventually a storm came to both men. The scripture says the rain came down, streams rose and winds blew and beat against both houses.

Here's the difference. I really want you to get this, so pay attention.

Although the storm was horrible. Although the winds were raging. It didn't faze the man who built his house on the rock. The house's foundation was grounded in that rock. That foundation was faith. It was belief. As a result, the wise man, as the Bible calls him, wasn't moved.

On the other hand, what do you think happened to the man who built his house on the sand—the "foolish man" as the scripture calls him?

The rain came down, the streams rose, the winds blew and eventually caused his house to crash because of his lack of foundation. His lack of faith. His lack of belief. His lack of a good attitude during the storm.

Two men. Same storm. One was wise enough to have a great foundation. The other didn't. His crib was wiped away because of it.

In the same way, when you're going through a difficult storm or trial, continue to speak TRIUMPH over that thang! Have some type of foundation. Don't get swept away in the storms of life. Withstand the damn storms! Stand strong! Firm!

Call things that are not as though they already are. Even if you have to talk to yourself, do it!

"I can handle it. It's not too hard me. If God allowed it then He's given me the strength to endure it. He's going to find a way to turn it around for my good."

You're strong. You're anointed for it. You're more than capable. Understand it may be a surprise to you, but it isn't a surprise to God. He isn't up there scratching his head, saying: "Oh man, what am I going to do? They got laid off. They're broke and can't pay their bills. I'm stomped."

No!

The key is to believe that He's working things out in your favor and to praise Him anyway, despite not seeing anything happening.

Many times when God is silent it means He's up in the heavens arranging things, working His butt off to turn things around in your favor. But you have to have faith.

And don't get me wrong — all of us doubt. Especially when you've prayed. You've believed. You're nice to people you don't even like. You've turned your cheek at work when a coworker tries to embarrass you. You've practically done everything humanly possible.

I totally understand. It's frustrating, but that's when, more than ever, you have to stir up your faith. Stir up your words. Release your faith.

You're more than a conqueror. You have can-do power. You're equipped with strength for the battle.

Speak TRIUMPH over that thang!

Dig deep. God has you in the palm of His hand. Realize it. Keep standing strong. Remind yourself this too shall pass — flat out.

God has NOT brought you this far to leave you.

Your words have creative power. You should know this by now from reading this book.

Your strength and power to overcome will disappear if you dwell on the negative, continuously complain and keep telling yourself you can't handle the storm.

Don't invite that junk into your spirit.

Know that God wouldn't allow the storm unless He has a divine purpose for it.

Trust Him even when it's difficult.

After you come out of the storm you'll be better off. You'll have more patience. Your ability to persevere will be off the chain. You'll step into a higher level of your destiny.

Joel Osteen once said in one of his messages: "Sometimes you face difficulties, not because you're doing something wrong, but because you're doing something right."

Don't get weary in well doing because you'll eventually reap the benefits if you don't give up!

Brothers and sisters, speak VICTORY in the middle of your storm. Your words matter during that time. If you continue speaking positive things, even when you don't see anything happening, your mourning will turn to joy. Your sadness into happiness. Don't worry. You got this!

CHAPTER 18: TRUSTING GOD WHEN IT DOESN'T MAKE SENSE

1 "Now a man named Lazarus was sick. He was from Bethany, the village of Mary and her sister Martha. 2 (This Mary, whose brother Lazarus now lay sick, was the same one who poured perfume on the Lord and wiped his feet with her hair). So the sisters sent word to Jesus, 'Lord, the one you love is sick.' 4 When he heard this, Jesus said, "This sickness will not end in death. No, it is for God's glory so that God's Son may be glorified through it."' 5 Now Jesus loved Martha and her sister and Lazarus. 6 So when he heard that Lazarus was sick, he stayed where he was two more days, 7 and then he said to his disciples, "Let us go back to Judea."
John 11:1-6

I think many of us can agree sometimes God just doesn't make sense. Like, not at ALL!

At one point in our lives, we've all sat back, scratched our heads and asked ourselves, "What in the world is going on in my life?" Things were shaking and all hell was breaking loose in every possible direction.

You prayed. You believed. But nothing happened. The situation didn't turn around. You didn't get the job. You didn't get the promotion. Your family member wasn't healed from cancer.

Then you thought to yourself, "God, you're God. You can easily turn this around. You know what I need. You know this bill needs to be paid. This just doesn't make sense!"

Am I right?

The scripture says Jesus stayed where he was two whole days when he received word Lazarus was sick.

Two!

I don't know about you, but that made no sense at the time. Why would Jesus decide to chill-out when Lazarus was in dire need of his help?

Bro, come on?

He wasn't too far away because Bethany was less than two miles from Jerusalem, at the most.

The scripture says Jesus loved Lazarus, Martha and Mary, but yet he still stayed put. How can you love someone, but stay put when they need your help? That's like me being sick with the flu. I call my momma to ask her to bring me orange juice and medicine, but she waits two whole days.

Huh? Who does that? I'd call the police for child neglect.

Just kidding. Moving on.

I can only imagine how Mary and Martha felt when Jesus didn't come to their aid, especially at a time when Lazarus was on his death bed.

I can hear Mary now. "Really, Jesus? I've poured oil on your feet and then washed it off with my long, beautiful hair and you're not going to do this simple thing for me? You trippin, bro."

But remember, God's ways aren't our ways.

Fast forward two days later. Jesus finally arrived, but Lazarus was dead as a result of the sickness. He was dead for four days and already had been put in a tomb. Martha goes out to meet Jesus, but Mary doesn't. She has an attitude with Jesus because if he hadn't been so late, Lazarus would still be living.

Mary decided to stay at home.

But again, God's ways aren't our ways.

As a matter of fact, Isaiah 55:8-9 puts it this way: 8 *"For my thoughts are not your thoughts, neither are your ways my ways," declares the LORD. 9 "As the heavens are higher than the earth, so are my ways higher than your ways and my thoughts than your thoughts."*

Jesus had something up his sleeve. Although Lazarus was dead in a physical sense, Jesus called it sleeping and his intentions were to wake him from his slumber.

Finally, Jesus asked where they had laid Lazarus. He then went over to his tomb. It was a cave with a stone rolled across the entrance. By this time, there was a stench to Lazarus' body because he had been in the tomb for so long.

You should know what happens next.

Jesus prayed and then commanded Lazarus to come out. He came out with his hands and feet wrapped in linen, and a cloth around his face.

Me personally, I would've passed out.

They went on to take the grave clothes off and the rest was history. Lazarus was alive and well again.

You see, Mary and Martha were thinking about a healing, but Jesus was thinking about a resurrection. At the time, they couldn't see it. They couldn't wrap their small minds around the fact that Lazarus was dead, Jesus was too late and that was that.

It made no sense for Jesus to sit still when Lazarus was on his death bed, none whatsoever.

But again, there was a method to his madness.

Jesus ended up bringing Lazarus back to life.

Friends, we have to learn how to trust God when He absolutely makes no sense. I know it's tough. I know it's frustrating. I know it's stressful. Most of all, I know it can be a burden. It feels like a huge weight is on your shoulders. A weight you can barely handle.

A weight that feels like it's going to crush you if it's not lifted off soon.

You're probably thinking, "Montezz, if God is sooo omnipotent. If he can stop any problem. If he can snap his fingers and cure any sickness. If he can increase my finances when I'm struggling in that area. Why won't He just do it already? Why?"

I don't know why. God is a mystery. There are plenty of scriptures in the Bible that say so.

Yes, it can be so annoying when you flat-out don't understand why God is allowing you and your family to go through hell.

Reverend Dr. Howard-John Wesley — who pastors Alfred Street Baptist Church in Alexandria, Virginia — said in one of his sermons, "Each and every one of us reaches some place in our life when what we go through doesn't match the image and the faith that you have in God."

Can I get an Amen on that one?

Brothers and sisters, what I've learned, and am still learning, is that we simply have to do one thing when God makes absolutely no sense — trust Him.

When you don't know where the money is going to come from to pay your bills, trust Him. When you keep getting rejected from jobs, trust Him. When you didn't get the promotion, trust Him. When you're broke, trust Him.

The key is to keep your words positive when you're in the middle of things that don't make sense.

That's when your faith is being released.

Psalms 19:14 says, 14 ***"May these words of my mouth and this meditation of my heart be pleasing in your sight, LORD, my Rock and my Redeemer."***

Your positive words — words of healing, words of faith — all of them please the man above, especially when things don't make sense.

Instead of complaining and saying things like, "I can't believe this is happening to me; it must not be meant for me to prosper, to be successful, to live an abundant life; this ain't fair; I give up," I need you to turn it around.

Say, "Lord, I know what I'm going through may be a surprise to me, but it's no surprise to you. Thank you for turning the situation around. I may not see anything happening yet, but I truly believe you're up there working things out in my favor.

"Thank you for my health. Thank you for my closed doors. Thank you for going before me, making my crooked places straight. I know in due time you'll work everything out for my good."

When you release your faith in this way, God instantly begins to go to work. He'll start turning things around in your favor.

It may not happen overnight, but restoration and deliverance will come before you know it.

But we have to continue to stay in faith. God can't operate if there's no faith. On the contrary, if your faith is as little as a mustard seed, you'll be able to overcome.

When God doesn't make sense, and you let it get to you, it'll affect your prayer life. You'll stop going to church. You'll get frustrated.

Some people may even curse Him because they just don't understand.

My friends, that's exactly what the enemy wants you to do. He wants you to give up believing in Him.

I've seen this my own life. Though I've mentioned this before, I feel the need to touch on it again.

I moved to Chicago in 2012 to attend graduate school. My beautiful aunt took me in out of the kindness of her heart. I graduated in 2014 with a Master of Arts in Journalism.

Unfortunately, my aunt passed away that next year from pancreatic cancer.

That didn't make sense.

I was working for a startup at the time making some pretty good money. Well, I was laid-off from that job the following year without warning.

Again, something that didn't make sense.

After being laid-off, I tried and tried and tried and tried to get another job. But it just wasn't happening for me for whatever reason. I eventually had to go on unemployment because of it. I was making a measly $514 every two weeks.

My bills were $1,400 per month. You do the math.

Didn't make sense.

During this process of finding a job, I'm helping others in their time of need — in particular, this one young lady who had just been let go from her TV reporting job. Even though we had attended the same graduate school, I never met her before.

One day she reached out to me on social media. Eventually we exchanged numbers. We got to know each other and became pretty good friends.

Many times she would call me crying because she was frustrated she wasn't landing anything. She'd say how she was losing faith in the Lord, how she couldn't take it anymore — just a little discouraged.

I continued to encourage her. I would tell her everything was going to be OK and that she was a talented reporter who was going to land a job very soon.

This went on for about five months or so.

While I'm encouraging her, I'm still trying to stay in faith myself. No jobs were calling me. None. Zero. Zilch. But it was all good. I was trying my best to stay in faith.

Finally, this young lady landed a job. I was so happy for her.

Me on the other hand, nothing. I was applying like she was. Reaching out to various news directors like she was. Even praying like she was.

Still nothing!

Yes, I was extremely happy for this young lady. I always want people to excel and prosper, but I must admit, I was frustrated.

I thought to myself, "Here I am encouraging and lifting the spirits of this girl I've never met. I'm praying she lands a job.

I'm comforting her. I'm doing this out of the kindness of my heart and I still can't land anything? Lord, why? What am I'm doing that's so wrong? What did I do? Why am I going through this?!"

It just didn't make sense.

Everyone around me was landing jobs —TV jobs, producing jobs, everything. I was searching just as hard. Praying just has hard. Believing just as hard. Yet, nothing was happening.

Friends, it's tough seeing others get promoted when you're working just as hard yourself to get promoted too.

It didn't make sense.

I felt like a low-life. I felt like a failure. I felt like I was letting everybody I knew down. The thing that was killing me deep down inside was that I wasn't even trying to be in that position. I was legitimately pursuing jobs, but couldn't land one to save my life!

I went on interview after interview after interview. Still nothing!

I was frustrated. I couldn't wrap my mind around what was happening to me. It just wasn't fair.

Most of all, IT DIDN'T MAKE SENSE!

One thing I wasn't going to do though was give up. I understood once you give up it'll all become permanent.

I kept applying.

Did my faith waver many times? Yes! Did I truly think about giving up? Sure did.

But no matter how many times I wanted to give up, I'd begin speaking those words of faith.

"Lord, this is frustrating. I don't understand it. It hurts. It's uncomfortable. But I know for a fact you have something big in store for me. I believe I can defy the odds and land a great gig. Something that will blow my mind. Thank you for what's coming my way. Thank you for working things out in my favor. It's only a matter of time."

It took me seven months to land a job.

Seven!

It felt like a weight had been lifted off of my shoulders.

God is the man!

Friends, trust Him. When God doesn't make sense, just trust Him. Yes, it's annoying. It's complicated. Many times it even hurts.

You've been praying, but don't see anything happening. Things are stagnant. Money is low. There's a delay. Trust Him.

A delay doesn't mean you're denied!

Keep in mind He wouldn't allow the difficulty to happen if there wasn't a DEVINE purpose for it. Sit still. Be productive. Everything will come together in due time.

There will be a time where you'll look back and realize why you went through what you went through.

Trust God When He Doesn't Make Sense!

CHAPTER 19: ARE YOUR FRIENDS SPEAKING THE RIGHT THINGS?

20 *"Walk with the wise and become wise, for a companion of fools suffers harm." Proverbs 13:20*

Are you surrounded by the right friends? Do they have goals and dreams, or are they stuck in mediocrity, not really doing anything with their lives?

As the saying goes, you become who you hang around the most.

If nine of your friends are broke, you'll become the tenth. If seven of your friends like to gossip, most likely you'll become the eighth. If six of your friends want to stay in mediocrity, it'll eventually rub off on you. Next thing you know you'll become the seventh, and then you'll settle for a life that's NOT God's best for you.

Of course there are exceptions, but many times that's how things go.

Your inner circle can give you a glimpse of what your future can possibly look like. This is why it's extremely important to have people around you whose counsel will guide you in the right direction instead of drag you down.

That's right — drag you down and crush your dreams.

Surround yourself with winners, doers instead of talkers. Surround yourself with friends who will uplift you, encourage you and tell you to shape up when you start getting off course. They should celebrate you when you come to them with unique ideas and dreams. They should be speaking nothing but faith and life into your future.

If your friends — your true friends — aren't doing this, then let me tell you. It's time to get some new ones.

If your friends are sarcastic, negative, dream killers who aren't pursuing anything in life, get rid of them.

Run and RUN fast!

Your destiny is too great and time is too valuable for you to waste your energy with negative friends. Friends who don't support your dreams. Friends who get intimidated with your current success or your future success. Friends who are unmotivated. Friends who tell you what you want to hear versus what you need to hear.

Surround yourself with happy friends, positive friends. Get around friends who'll never steer you wrong; who will challenge you.

Your inner circle of friends should be consistent, intellectual, goal-oriented and godly.

Period!

Remember: you are the sum of the people you hang around on a daily basis.

What are your friends speaking over your life? How are they help-ing to shape your future? What are they doing to help move you closer to your destiny?

Again, keep this scripture in mind: 17 *"As iron sharpens iron, so one person sharpens another." Proverbs 27:17*

Joel Osteen once said in one of his sermons: "You can't hang around with chickens and expect to soar with eagles."

Or in the words of the great Les Brown: "Birds of a feather flock together. If you run around with losers, you will end up a loser."

Listen to what your friends are saying to you. They should be speaking nothing but favor, prosperity and faith into your spirit. They should be challenging you, uplifting you. They should check you when you're not on top of your game, or if they see that you're becoming lazy.

If your inner circle of friends — I mean the closest ones to you — are telling you what you can't accomplish — that your dreams are too big and there's no way they can come true. If they belittle you for what God put in your heart. I say this respectively, throw up the deuces. Get some new friends.

You're not going to become all you were created to be if you continue to hang around bad friends.

Yes, if you grew up with them I understand how hard it can be to move forward without them. Remember, though, everybody can't go where God is taking you.

Look at it like a bus route. People riding the bus will get off at various stops along the route.

You're the driver of the bus. Your life is the bus. You're in control of it.

Imagine your friends as the passengers.

Whether you like it or not, many of your friends will have to get dropped off at certain stops because they can't go where God is taking you. They just can't! And He knows it.

They can't go because they'll hinder you instead of help you.

I'm not saying cut your friends off immediately. I'm also not saying you should forget where you came from as you climb higher and higher.

No. Never that.

I'm simply telling you to gradually cut off the ones who are toxic. Do it one day at a time. Stop spending so much time with them. Reduce it little by little.

You're probably saying, "Well Montezz, I don't want to be lonely. It takes time to meet new friends. I don't want to be looked at as fake."

Brothers and sisters, it's better to go through a season of loneliness than to miss your destiny. Stay in faith and God will bring better friends across your path; more fulfilling friends.

If you don't get the wrong friends out of your life, you'll never meet the right ones.

You don't have to be rude. There shouldn't be this huge announcement made. No, just start distancing yourself one day at a time.

Friends, spirits are transferrable.

If you hang out with gossipers, you'll end up a gossiper. If you hang out with thieves, you'll become a thief. If you spend time around critical fault-finders, you'll become a critical, fault-finding person. If you hang around complainers, sure enough, you'll eventually turn into a complainer.

On the other hand, imagine if your friends were just the opposite.

If you hang around people of excellence, you better believe excellence will rub off on you. Their success will motivate you to become successful.

If you're hanging around with smart business men or women, you'll begin to develop a business-like mind.

If you hang around with generous people, you'll become more generous.

We have to be selective with who we spend our time with.

You need eagles in your life, not chickens. Get friends who are going places in life. Friends who are motivated and looking to change the world. Before long, those qualities will rub off on you.

My mentor, the great Rob Parker, has reached a certain level of success in his career. He has been on national TV with some amazing personalities. He has also made appearances on national radio shows.

His success inspires me to be great. I always keep in contact with him. He gives me a lot of valuable advice.
He's just an overall great mentor.

Because of it, I have it made up in my mind that I refuse to settle for mediocrity. I refuse to settle for less than God's best.

You should too!

Set boundaries for your life.

The scripture says, 14 *"Do not set foot on the path of the wicked or walk in the way of evildoers. 15 Avoid it, do not travel on it; turn from it and go on your way." Proverbs 4:14-15*

Don't spend time with friends who bring out the worst in you. If you're always having to defend yourself, argue and compromise, that's a sure sign you're surrounded by the wrong friends. Your friends should be sharpening you. Making you better.

Understand you can also outgrow friends too; ones you may have known since you were born.

That friend may have been your right hand. The two of you would always hang around one another. Go out. Travel. The whole nine.

But it's just not the same anymore. Life has caused you to think differently. Pursue different careers. Different paths. It's just not the same like back in the day. The season has changed.

You've outgrown one another.

There's nothing wrong with it. It doesn't necessarily make that friend a bad person.

Not at all.

It simply means the season is over. That particular friend was ordained to be in your life for a certain amount of time and now that time may be over.

Listen to the signs. Don't miss your destiny because you want to be stuck with a friend or friends that aren't doing you any good.

That's called being a people pleaser.

One of the hardest things to do is to let go of people we know aren't supposed to be in our lives anymore. This is especially true when it's friends that we grew up with.

You'll have to love some of your friends from a distance. Their place in your life adds no value anymore.

Make sure you separate yourself from them little by little.

Here's another thought. Stop telling your dreams to small-minded friends. You know the ones I'm talking about. The ones that instantly tell you, "That's a dumb idea. You can never do that. You don't have the money. You don't have the experience. That idea will never work."

If you hear those things — run!

Not everybody can handle your dreams. Everybody won't be able to see it. God put the dream in your heart, not in the heart of your critics.

It's unfortunate to say, but even some of your family members can be dream killers.

Take the story of Joseph for example. His story began in the first book of the Bible, Genesis, chapter 37. For those who aren't familiar with the story of Joseph let me put you on game real quick.

Kick back and peep the story.

Joseph was 17-years-old. He was the youngest of ten children. Joseph's brothers were jealous of him because, according to Genesis 37:3 — Jacob, their father — 3 *"loved Joseph more than any of his sons, because he had been born to him in his old age; and he made an ornate robe for him."*

Jacob loved Joseph so much that he made him a special robe to make him standout.

Verse four goes on to say: 4 ***"When his brothers saw that their father loved him more than any of them, they hated him and could not speak a kind word to him."***

Ladies and gents, the spirit of jealousy literally kills. It's a strong emotion. And it can lead you to kill someone if you're not careful!

Think about how many men and women kill their spouse because of jealousy.

One day, Joseph had two unique dreams. He told his brothers about them.

I mean, he went in full detail, y'all. I want you to keep in mind that his brothers already hated him because their father loved him the most!

Here's what he said...

6 ***"Listen to this dream I had: We were binding sheaves of grain out in the field when suddenly my sheaf rose and stood upright, while your sheaves gathered around mine and bowed down to it." Genesis 37:6***

His second dream...

9 ***"Then he had another dream, and he told it to his brothers. 'Listen,' he said, 'I had another dream, and this time the sun and moon and eleven stars were bowing down to me." Genesis 37:9***

Their reaction was horrible. No support at all. Nothing but negativity flowed out of their mouths. No, I should say out of their hearts, since your mouth says whatever flows out of your heart.

Friends, you can't tell everybody your goals and dreams. Even if it's a family member.

Joseph's brothers hated him because of what he had told them. Pure disrespect is how they took it. Their impression of Joseph was that he thought he was above them. He wanted to reign over them. But that wasn't the case.

One day, his brothers were plotting to kill him, but decided against it when the oldest, Rueben, overheard their plan. Instead, Rueben told the rest of the brothers not to take his life, but to throw him into a pit. After throwing him into a pit they planned on telling their father an animal ate him. They were flat-out hating.

Mind you, this is all over a dream.

16 *"For where you have envy and selfish ambition, there you find disorder and every evil practice." James 3:16*

Eventually they ended up throwing Joseph into that pit.

It didn't end there.

Not too long after, some people came by who wanted to sell some things in Egypt. That gave Joseph's brothers the bright idea to sell him into slavery instead of shedding his blood.

All of the brothers agreed and proceeded to sell Joseph into slavery. He was sold to an important man by the name of Potiphar.

Potiphar was Pharaoh's official — the captain of the guard.

This is how the Lord works.

Potiphar eventually put Joseph in control of everything he owned — even his household.

Then things took a horrible turn.

The Bible says Joseph was handsome and well-built. So yes, ladies, you would've loved him.

One day, Potiphar's wife took notice of it and wanted to sleep with him. He turned her down. She kept asking again and again. Day after day. Joseph kept refusing. He never fell into the trap.

However, on this one particular try, Joseph slipped up. He did the right thing by running away, but he made the mistake of leaving his cloak with her.

Potiphar's wife lied and said Joseph tried to sleep with her, using his cloak as false proof.

Potiphar got furious and threw him into prison for over 10 years.

Again, all of this is because of the dreams he revealed to his brothers.

But this is how God works.

Joseph was put in charge of some prisoners.

Favor.

Fast forward, Joseph was let out of prison. He got the chance to interpret two dreams for the Pharaoh when he was released. His interpretation of Pharaoh's dreams was that Egypt would have seven years of abundance followed by seven years of famine.

Pharaoh was so impressed he put Joseph in charge of the entire land of Egypt.

After the first seven years were up, a famine hit Egypt just like Joseph had predicted. It lasted for seven years. The struggle was real.

Joseph's interpretations were coming true.

The good news was that Joseph had stored up lots of food during the abundant years, especially grain.

As a result, people from all around the world began buying grain from Joseph.

Checkout how God works things out for your good.

Word spread fast. Jacob got the news and sent his 10 sons to Egypt to buy grain so they wouldn't starve to death. The only son Jacob didn't send on the journey was Benjamin — the youngest — because he was worried he wouldn't return.

How could you blame him? Jacob had seen this movie before.

Since Joseph was in charge of all the land in Egypt, he was in control of selling all the grain to his people.

One day, Joseph's brothers came before him to buy grain. They bowed down to him just like he had saw in his dream. His brothers didn't recognize him, but he sure recognized them. But Joseph pretended not to know them.

Joseph asked where they were from. They told him. And then he remembered his dreams.

After some time had passed — and yes, after some harsh treatment toward his brothers — Joseph eventually came to his senses and made himself known. He forgave his brothers. They repaired their relationship and then Joseph moved them, along with their father, out to Egypt.

They inherited some of the best land in Egypt, living lavishly in the middle of a famine.

Joseph went from the pit, to prison, to the PALACE, all because of two dreams.

See, Joseph should've kept his mouth shut about the dreams he had. This is a perfect lesson of how things can take a bad turn when you tell a big dream to small-minded people. It didn't matter if those small-minded people were his own brothers.

Instead of congratulating Joseph — their own flesh and blood — they instantly shot down his dreams with no hesitation. They didn't even try to give the kid a chance to explain. Because of hatred and jealousy, they interpreted Joseph's dreams as a sign of disrespect. Their little minds couldn't grasp the fact that they would bow down to their brother one day, not knowing that the bowing down would in turn become a blessing and change their lives forever.

Joseph didn't mean anything by it when he told them his dreams. After all, he was the youngest child, just 17-years-old. He didn't know better. Plus, he felt he was just telling his family. People he could trust.

Friends, you can't go around telling everybody your dreams. Unfortunately, sometimes you can't even tell your own family.

Joseph went through all of that pain simply because he had two dreams and then revealed them to the wrong people.

But God is faithful. Everything came to pass

Comedian, actor and writer, Steve Harvey, made the mistake of telling his big dream to a small-minded person too. It was his grade school teacher.

Harvey's dream was always to be on TV. He just knew deep down inside he was going to have his own show someday.

Mind you, this was in the 60s, a time when racism was still pretty crazy.

One day, Harvey's teacher told the class to write what they wanted to be when they grew up on a piece of paper.

Harvey put down he wanted to be on television.

The teacher told Harvey to go in the front of the class and then tell everybody what he wrote down on that sheet of paper. Harvey stood up and said again, "I want to be on TV."

Here's this little black kid with child-like faith, who had a huge dream of being on the TV screen.

The teacher looked at him crazy and asked did he know anybody that has ever been on TV.

Young Harvey said no.

She shot down his dream, immediately. She didn't believe in it. This teacher told him all the reasons why he couldn't be on TV.

Friends, one thing you should never do is shoot down a child's dream.

1"A gentle answer turns away wrath, but a harsh word stirs up anger." Proverbs 15:1

The teacher told Harvey to go home, tell his parents what he wrote on the sheet of paper, change it and then bring it back to school.

There was no way he could be on TV. That's what she thought. There's no way this black kid can achieve something like that.

When he got home he explained what happened in class that day. His mother told his father what he wrote on the paper.

His father asked him, "What did you write on that paper, boy?" Harvey replied with passion: "I want to be on TV!"

His mother suggested Harvey's father should whoop his butt for writing something like that on the paper.

Harvey's father asked him why he would write something like that on the piece of paper. Harvey told him, "Because that's what the teacher asked me."

Then his father asked again: "Well, what did you put on the paper boy?" Harvey: "I want to be on TV."

His father looked at his wife and said, "Well, what's wrong with that?"

Just like Joseph, Harvey received so much backlash because he had a dream.

Harvey's father then looked at his wife and said, "This boy can be on TV if he wants to be."

Her response: "No, he has to write what that teacher told him to put on that piece of paper."

Harvey's father told him to go into his room. Harvey thought to himself, "Hell, I'm about to get my butt whooped anyway. What do I have to lose?"

Here's the kicker. Words, my friends, words. Words of encouragement. Words of life. Words of faith. You never know how they can change someone's life.

Harvey's father walked into the room and asked him what the teacher wanted him to write on the paper.

You see, since she couldn't see the dream God put in his heart, she automatically put him into a box and limited what she thought he could achieve in his life.

The teacher suggested he put a police officer, something more realistic.

Harvey's father then told him to take the piece of paper with "policeman" on it to his dream-killing teacher at school.

Then he ordered him to keep the paper with "I want to be on TV" and stash it in his dresser. Harvey's father said he wanted young Harvey to read the piece of paper every morning and night. He told him to keep the faith, keep believing in his dream and go after it.

Those words of counsel. Words of advice. Wise words. They changed young Harvey for the better.

He kept his dream in front of him from that point forward. No matter how many times he slipped up. No matter how many detours he took. Even being homeless between ages 30-33, he always kept the faith, knowing that one day he'd have his own show.

Don't be that person. Don't shoot down someone's dream just because you can't see it for yourself. You never know what a person can achieve.

Besides family, your friends should be your number one fan! They shouldn't be intimidated by your potential. They should speak nothing but prosperity, life and blessings over you. They should congratulate you when you do something big in life — accomplish a goal, get a degree. If it's a positive accomplishment they should praise you.

Take a look at your friends. Are they a good reflection of you? Are they dreamers or dream killers? Are they speaking the right things over your life? Are they even speaking the right things over their own lives?

Are they?

If not, you have some serious thinking to do. Your cut-off game has to become a bit strong.

Words have so much power. They can cause you to triumph or give up. Speak nothing but triumph over your friends.

There are so many cases in the world where people have given up on their dreams because of what someone has spoken over their life.

Wherever you go, there will be dream killers. But it really hits home when it's your own family and friends. There's something about their words that cut a little deeper than the words of strangers.

If a stranger tells you you'll never make it, you'll never become successful, it's a bit easier to recover from rather than when your close family or friends are the ones saying those things. It stings that much more.

Don't be that person.

Again, **IRON SHARPENS IRON.**

CHAPTER 20: MY LAST THOUGHTS

11 "The mouth of the righteous is a fountain of life, but the mouth of the wicked conceals violence." Proverbs 10:11

Unfortunately, I've come to the end of my book. That's right my friends, this is the final chapter. If I say so myself, it's been a great journey. Before I go though, I want to share my last thoughts with you.

Brothers and sisters, you're a child of the most high God. Let your light shine wherever you go. Not only should your light brighten up those around you, make sure you never let yours dim. The day it dims is the day you start to die.

Please, I beg of you, **Watch Your Words.** Watch what you say about yourself. Be conscience of what you're saying about your future. Be aware of the blessings or curses you're speaking over your own life. Your words have more power than you can ever imagine. Train your tongue to spew only good and wholesome things. Train your tongue to encourage instead of discourage. Build up rather than tear down.

Speak prosperity and abundance instead of lack.

We live in a cruel, cruel world. A world where most people are out for themselves. A world where many people are motivated by money, greed, power, status and deceit. A world where people are willing to do anything to get ahead — even if it means stepping on your shoes to get there.

That's why Psalms 37:1-2 says, *1"Do not fret because of those who are evil or be envious of those who do wrong; 2 for like the grass they will soon wither, like green plants they will soon die away."*

The world is the devil's playground, literally. He has come to kill, steal and devour anyone in his path.

My prayer is that you don't fall into the trap of conforming to the idolatries of this world.

No!

Like the scripture says, don't "**be envious of those who do wrong...**" It's not worth it.

Philippians 2:3-4 says, *3"**Do nothing out of selfish ambition or vain conceit. Rather, in humility, value others above yourselves,** 4 **not looking to your own interests but each of you to the interests of the others."**

Pay attention to what you're saying. Many of us have been speaking negative things for so long that it has become second nature. We've become numb to it. It's like a muscle we've been working out constantly at the gym.

Let me reiterate what Paul said in Ephesians. 29 "**Do not let any unwholesome talk come out of your mouths, but only what is helpful for building others up according to their needs that it may benefit those who listen." Ephesians 4:29**

He went on to say in verses 31 and 32: 31 "**Get rid of all bitterness, rage and anger, brawling and slander, along with every form of malice.** 32 **Be kind and compassionate to one another, forgiving each other, just as in Christ God forgave you."**

Even back then, over 2,000 years ago, Paul knew the importance of using your words wisely.

Let me ask you. Are your words beneficial to others? Or are they hurtful? Are you stirring up strife?

Friends, you can't go off of your emotions. Learn how to control them. Think about what you're going to say. Never let your tongue run wild.

Do you know how many headaches you can save yourself from if you were to watch your words?

The reason why we have two ears and one mouth is because we should listen more than we talk.

Checkout James 1:19: 19 *"My dear brothers and sisters, take note of this: Everyone should be quick to listen, slow to speak and slow to become angry, because human anger does not produce the righteousness that God desires."*

Here are two more powerful scriptures about your tongue. I've mentioned these before, but I think it's necessary to use it again in order to drive my point home.

5 "Likewise, the tongue is a small part of the body, but it makes great boasts. Consider what a great forest is set on fire by a small park. 6 The tongue also is a fire, a world of evil among the parts of the body. It corrupts the whole body, sets the whole course of one's life on fire, and is itself set on fire by hell." James 3:5-6

The scripture says the tongue *"is a fire, a world of evil..."* if it's used incorrectly. I'm challenging you to use it in a good way.

Let me give you an example.

I remember one day after church I decided to go to a nice Mexican restaurant for lunch. It was literally right around the corner. When I got there, I sat at the bar instead of at a table. Within minutes of sitting down I said to myself "Hmmm...instead of eating lunch I think I can go for a margarita or two."

Is that bad given the fact that it was right after church?

OK. That's neither here nor there.

While I'm finishing my first lime margarita, a woman randomly came up to me and sparked a conversation. She asked me what kind of margarita I was drinking. I told her. Then she suggested I try a cucumber one.

My face frowned up because I'm not a huge cucumber fan, only when I'm eating them in a salad can I tolerate them.

That's what I told her.

She insisted that I try a cucumber margarita. I denied once again saying, "No. No. I'm good. I just don't think I'll like it."

She was full-blooded Mexican. A Latina. Shoutout to my Latina's in the world!!!

Moving on…

Finally, I gave in. She bought me a small cucumber margarita on the rocks. I tried it and it was fantastic. I was appalled.

She was absolutely right!

I was flat-out wrong. She basically said, "I told you so" in so many words and then went back to her table.

After about 20 minutes, this young lady called my name, telling me to come join her and her friend at their table. I accepted and walked over. We made small talk. They asked me where I was from, how I liked Chicago, etc.

Then the conversation got serious. Something happened. Out of nowhere, the young lady's friend started telling me how she was battling kidney stones and was in constant pain from time to time, even while we were chilling at the table.

This friend was celebrating her birthday.

Instantly, something began to rise up in my spirit. I wanted to speak nothing but life and health over her.

Nothing else!

I started saying things to this affect: "You're healthy. Your body is healing. You're going to be just fine. Don't worry. Everything will be OK. Your kidneys will continue to work perfectly normal. No sickness will last in your body. It's leaving. It's over. Instead of thinking about the pain, think about your healing. Think about good health. Great health is coming unto you!"

This lady began to cry at the table. I could tell she had never had a random guy who she'd just met speak such encouraging words over her life.

She absolutely couldn't believe it.

My words were penetrating her spirit as tears were flowing from her beautiful eyes. This lady needed to hear those words, badly. God put it on my heart to speak such positive things over her life.

Imagine if it would've been the total opposite? Imagine if I decided to discourage her instead of uplift her spirits? Imagine if I would've said something to this extent: "Wow. That sounds horrible. Kidney stones are pretty serious. You need to go back to the doctor. You may not ever get well. Good luck with that!"

See the difference? It's like night and day. Just by reading it, it makes you feel bad inside. Talk about a poor choice of words.

My encouraging words caused her to not only cry, but she began to laugh. She began to show that pretty smile of hers.

Her spirits had been lifted!

The story doesn't stop there. More things began to happen.

The original friend who called me over to sit at the table began to tell how she was heartbroken. She was a mother of two and had recently gotten divorced because she found out her husband was cheating on her.

This lady was 42-years-old, way older than me.

As she was telling me this, tears began to fall from her face as well. I took a tissue and started wiping her tears since she was sitting right next to me.

When she was finished telling me her story, I began to uplift her spirits.

I said: "Not to worry. I know it hurts seeing someone whom you love very much cheat on you. Most of all, I know it's tough going through a divorce, although I've never been through one myself.

"I do understand hurt and pain though. But, everything will work out for the good. You're a great woman, a smart woman, a very attractive woman. Don't fret over what was. Don't fret over the past. Move forward. Don't get stuck. Everything will be OK. Your children need you to be strong."

Now let's turn that situation around.

Imagine if I said these things instead: "Your husband did what? What did you do to make him cheat on you? You had to do something. Maybe it's you. Maybe you didn't love him enough. I'd think about what you did and then try to fix it."

She probably would've slapped me, spilled the pitcher of margaritas on me and then told me to get out even though she didn't own the restaurant!

Brothers and sisters, I didn't know those two women from a grain of sand. My first time meeting them was after church in this particular restaurant. And I may not ever see them again either.

What are the odds of that happening?

God has a way of using you to help people. He has a way of directing our footsteps so we can be a blessing to others.
I truly believe that's what happened that day.

God knew they needed to hear words of healing and encouragement. He already knew they needed to hear words that would lift their spirits. He anointed me to be that guy and I didn't even know it.

How did I go from a conversation about trying a different type of margarita to encouraging two women where one was battling a sickness and the other battling an emotional divorce?

Friends, God works in mysterious ways!

Again, I can't stress this enough. Be careful what you speak over people. Make an effort to make a person's day. You never know what people are going through. Our words can easily destroy someone's self-esteem.

Don't be that person.

The same goes for your finances, your career, your children, your health, your relationships — even your trials and tribulations.

Your words matter. Remember, life and death is in the power of the tongue.

Furthermore, I want you all to cast down negative, discouraging words. Don't entertain them. Refuse them. Don't dwell on the lies.

People will speak negative things over your life. It's inevitable. But you can't let that poison get on the inside. If you do, before long you'll start believing it. And once you start believing it, that's when the enemy has you. It'll create a stronghold in your mind.

Never listen to discouraging words of defeat.

Never!

The scripture says we will have to give an account for every idle word that we've spoken. That means you shouldn't say everything that's on your mind.

Better yet, here's the scripture: 36 *"But I tell you that everyone will have to give account on the day of judgment for every empty word they have spoken. 37 For by your words you will be acquitted, and by your words you will be condemned."* *Matthew 12:36-37*

People who choose to speak words of discouragement and curses over your life will eventually fall into their own pit. You can't worry about it. You have to be mentally strong and have thick skin.

Many people don't understand that we tend to heal more quickly from physical scars than verbal scars. It's simply because the words will go deep down inside of your spirit if you allow them to. And then if you're not careful, they'll stick to you like fatty foods.

Don't let them stick. Go on a diet. A God diet!

Brothers and sisters, who do yo believe? The report of God or the report of man? God says nothing but good things about you and your life. Man doesn't.

God says you're an overcomer. Man doesn't. God says you can do all things. Man says you're limited and you lack talent. God says whatever you touch will succeed. Man says you're a failure and you'll never be good enough.

Who do you believe? The report of man or the report of your creator?

Whenever you're trying to make a difference in the world, people will always try to come against you. They'll try to break your spirits with their cruel words and lack of faith in you.

Don't let that stop you. Don't let the words penetrate your spirit.

Ignore them!

You have greatness within you. You haven't even discovered the things you can do yet. In order for you to tap into that power you have to ignore the negative words people speak over you.

It's a must!

Do you know how many times people have told me I'm not good enough? That I couldn't make it?

At times, I was so tempted to believe them. I would think to myself, "Maybe they're right. Maybe that's the reason why I haven't gotten the job I want in broadcasting. Maybe I'm not talented. Maybe I don't have what it takes."

Eventually I would stop in my tracks and erase those dumb thoughts because that's exactly what they are — dumb! I had to realize just because I'm not getting offers doesn't mean I'm not good enough.

Joyce Meyer once said in one of her sermons, "A delay is not a denial."

She's right!

Those of you who have big dreams and goals, don't give up. Just because it's not happening as fast as you thought, it doesn't mean it's not going to happen.

In the middle of chasing your dreams, remember to pick and choose your words wisely. If you continue to say to yourself, "It's never going to happen. I'll never reach my dreams. It's taking too long. I don't have what it takes." You'll eventually believe it yourself and throw in the towel like a boxer getting his butt whooped.

No! Stop it!

You'll believe more of what you say about yourself than what others speak over you.

Continue to call things that are not as though they already are.

That's the key.

Are there going to be rough patches? Of course. Tough times? Of course. Times when you're going to want to quit? Sure.

Giving up is NOT an option for you. You're strong, talented, smart, creative, intellectual and thought-provoking.

Steve Harvey was homeless for three years. Les Brown was taking baths in his office building. The both of them are successful.

Don't feed into the lies the enemy is whispering in your ear. Combat that negativity with words of life, joy, prosperity and faith!

One last note.

Many of us know famous comedian and actor, Kevin Hart. We see his success today, but we don't understand what he had to go through to get there.

Hart started at a small comedy club in his hometown of Philadelphia, Pennsylvania. He was raised by a single mother because his father was on drugs and spent more time in jail than out.

Hart's first stage name was Lil' Kev the Bastard.

He bombed plenty of shows. I'm talking about BOMBED!

People didn't find him funny, but he kept working hard. He kept working on his dream. He stayed true to himself. He knew if he continued to work hard and not give up, his dreams would eventually come true.

"Everybody wants to be famous, but nobody wants to put in the work," he says.

Hart faced rejection after rejection time and time again. I'm pretty sure he got discouraged at times, but that was no reason for him to throw in the towel.

Instead, he just kept working on his craft, trying to be the best version of himself that he could possibly be.

He continued to encourage himself even though he was broke and his mother had to help pay his rent.

His words remained positive. He continued to speak great things into the atmosphere, knowing without a doubt his dreams were eventually going to become a reality.

And they did!

He eventually blew up. Hart made over $28.5 million in 2015 and upwards of $87.5 million in 2016.

Talk about living in overflow. My goodness. This didn't happen by accident though. It wasn't luck.

That's what continuing to believe in yourself will do for you. That's why no matter the circumstances, you don't faint or give up when things get tough. That's why you continue to let positive words come out of your mouth.

Imagine if Hart began speaking defeat.

He would've eventually talked himself out of his own dreams. He would've never reached success.

Never!

Now he's reaping the benefits of hard work, confidence, positive words, listening to mentors, studying the greats, the whole nine.

If he can do it, you can too!

Brothers and sisters, WATCH YOUR WORDS. They have the ability to bless or curse, uplift or degrade, encourage or discourage, build or tear down.

Your words have creative power. Whatever you're saying about yourself, your situation, your career, etc., your life will eventually flow in that direction.

Don't let it happen. Be conscience of what you're saying to yourself and others.

You have what it takes. You have greatness within you.

WATCH YOUR WORDS.

Peace,

Montezz Allen

Thanks For Reading!

1 Peter 3:8-12

8 Finally, all of you, be like-minded, be sympathetic, love one another, be compassionate and humble. 9 Do not repay evil with evil or insult with insult.
On the contrary, repay evil with blessing, because to this you were called so that you may inherit a blessing. 10 For,
"Whoever would love life and see good days must keep their tongue from evil and their lips from deceitful speech. 11 They must turn from evil and do good;
they must seek peace and pursue it. 12 For the eyes of the Lord are on the righteous and his ears are attentive to their prayer, but the face of the Lord is against those who do evil."

Watch Your Words

Made in the USA
Columbia, SC
12 September 2020